Cake Biz Success

Diana – The Cake Biz Coach

Contents

Chapter 1 : Realising Your Cake Dream

Your Cake Business Success Dream, Vision and Goal

Congratulations you have taken your first step to realising your dream of owning and running a successful cake business.

I will tell you right from the start that you can do this, the only limitations to you not being successful in the cake business is YOU!

Owning a successful cake business is not a dream it is a goal.

You may already be running a cake business from home, or you are a hobby caker whose friends and family love your cakey creations so much that you want to do this professionally, or you could be at the start of your journey into cake business. It matters not, this book is to help show you the way to realising your dream.

This book may not be what you are expecting a book about running a cake business to be, but if it is success in the cake business you want then I will use my tried and tested techniques and get you there.

This book is written with love and passion in order that I can pass on all that I have learned in my years in the cake business and as a business coach.

I make no apologies for this being a 'go hard or go home' cake business book, as I am serious about helping you to make a success of your cake business.

It truly breaks my heart to see and hear from fellow caker's that they are still haggling with potential cake customers over prices, and burning the midnight oil to complete orders. I want this to be a book where you step back and look at your cake business now, and compare it to what you really want from a successful cake business.

If you haven't started your cake business yet now is the time to sit back, read the book and focus on planning a successful cake business from the get-go.

So I will start straight away. Here in chapter one, getting you match fit for the journey ahead to achieving success in the cake business.

Again it matters not that you haven't yet baked a cake, honestly, or if you have been running a cake business for years, let's focus today on you being in the premier league of cake businesses and not plodding along possibly earning close to the minimum wage (I kid you not), being stressed and burnt out, trying to get those cakes finished … that all stops here!

Straight away I will show you the four main ingredients you need to run a successful cake business

I don't want you to be busy fools, known as the go-to cheap cake person in town!

So here it is chapter one your four main ingredients to success in the cake business, and no you won't find them in your pantry or at the supermarket.

These main ingredients I liken to your flour, eggs, butter, and sugar .....

(Later I will also talk a little about the barriers that maybe will prevent you from achieving your cake business success unless you identify and deal with them now.)

So let's dive straight in and look at the ' Four Main Ingredients to Success In the Cake Business.

1. Set your Goal
2. Create your Vision
3. Focus daily on your Goal & Vision
4. Learn daily.

Not what you expected? My methods of getting you there may differ from other coaches or mentors, but they get results.

Firstly you must believe that you will be running a successful cake business, and most importantly living the life you dream of because you're running a successful cake business.

Later in the book I will talk to you about the other ingredients you need, such as effective marketing, how to confidently charge your worth for your cakes, how to find and retain your ideal cake customers etc., but first we need to lay down a solid foundation for you to work from and it's your vision of success and your goal.

1. So let's create your GOAL...

Your dream of the life you want to lead, as a result of running a successful cake business, doesn't have to include owning a yacht in St Tropez, or climbing aboard your own personal liar jet (as this may not be achievable for even the best cake business owner in the world).

Your dream of success in the cake business is personal to you, it is your dream of the life you want to live when you are running a successful cake business.

Your dream may be to become a household name in the cake business, whatever it is, it is your dream and your goal.

Just Google the top ten successful cake business owners in the UK, and look at them carefully.

They were you once.... honestly. They had a dream, and now they may have achieved their success goal, or maybe not!

They may still be on their journey and their vision of success in the cake business may be different to yours.

I am sure of one thing though, that they achieved their vision of running a successful cake business with a goal, a clear vision and a commitment to continually developing by learning.

It may have taken them a short time or longer than they expected to achieve a successful cake business, and some of them are well-known names in cake circles, but this could be you. There is no reason why it can't be.

Success means different things to different people it is not always about earning thousands of pounds, or it might be. It is important at the start to work out the why you want to be successful in the cake business

So in order to outline your goal answer me this question now:
Why Do I Want to Be Successful in The Cake Business?
Once you have answered this question you have the foundations to take you on your journey to your cake business success and you have a clear GOAL, a reminder every day to focus you on why you are doing what you are doing with your cake business.

Your answer might be:

To step off the 9 x 5 hamster wheel in order to actually be there to take my kids to school, or if you are already running a cake business it may be to work less and earn good money.
To be able to spend more time caring for elderly relatives.
To have the freedom to travel when I like and not be constrained by only four weeks annual leave a year.
It may be health reasons.

All of the above are some of the main reasons my previous 'Cake Biz 'students, my 'Cakepreneurs', have given me for wanting to run a successful cake business.

All of the above isn't about earning millions, they are about earning enough to provide, or replace. a good income whilst giving them flexibility and a quality of life.

Now go and get an A4 piece of paper and write your GOAL in capitals on it. Put this title in big letters along the top.

'Running a Successful Cake Business will give me ..... '

Once you have written your goal maybe put this on your fridge or somewhere at eye level.

You may want to skip the above, as you may not be one of those 'showy' people, and believe me I understand, but bear with me on this one, and go and do it now! If not the fridge a prominent place where you and your household can see it.

There could be hundreds of other reasons you could put down but be careful there is a wrong reason, and that is to earn lots of money and be rich!

Putting this down as your goal for your cake business will not be helpful at all, trust me on this one.

You see moving away from an issue, maybe you have got yourself a bit behind, and in debt and you want to earn extra cash by setting up a cake business whilst you are working in another job

You see wanting lots of money and wanting to be rich is usually, but not always, associated with an issue such as debt or a lack of money.

Setting money as your goal is moving away from an issue and proven not to be as successful as working towards a goal like, I want to live in a bigger house so the kids have more room.

The bigger house is the goal to work towards and visualise, a happy goal!

I am not saying that ' to make more money ' this isn't a good reason to start a cake business, I am just pointing out that you are more likely to be a success in the cake business if you have a clear positive goal to work towards in your future by running a successful cake business.

It has been shown that if you turn away from the issue and face and focus on your vision, your goal, of what success in the cake business means for you, you are more likely to achieve success.

Maybe that picture of a happier more content family, relaxing family or leisure time at the gym or on holiday, or that bigger house.

Being rich and focusing on money will not help your mind focus and run towards your goal, so if money was your answer to the above question, try again to think of another reason, which isn't about money.

So you have your goal, a positive reason why you want to run a successful cake business, now it's time to visualise your success.

2. Create your VISION ….

As I said previously, in psychological terms working towards a vision is believed to be more powerful than having the willpower to move away from an issue like I'm not making enough money from my cakes.

I want you to visualise what success means to you. (I am a great believer in vision boards to help you visualise, whether that be creating one as your screensaver on your laptop or phone, and or putting a pictorial representation of your vision/goal in a frame and on the wall or on the fridge. Somewhere you can see it daily.)

There is lots of information on vision boards on the internet, and they are very powerful tools if used correctly in business.

Just one thing left to put on or in your vision board and that is a picture of a happy you. it's you in that scene living that successful life as a result of running a successful cake business.

Go on, cut round a picture of yourself and stick it on that beach, maybe with your partner or the kids, those that you want to be in this successful life as a result of running a business.

3.   Focus daily on your Goal & Vision

In any business, especially the cake business, there are lots of things that can distract us and take us off course. Unless you can focus on your goal and vision of what being successful in the cake business looks like to you will wander off course, believe me.

So look at your goal and vision daily, breathe it in and let it set you up for your day ahead.

I do not apologise for the very uncakey mindset techniques I use in this chapter, which I learnt in my study of the psychology of success, as I truly believe that it is this that has helped me in business and helped me help others to be successful through my cake business coaching programs, and therefore I feel I must share it with you.

I do employ these techniques as they are proven to help you be successful in your cake business, but I won't blind you with the science or the labels behind it ... promise.

I will talk later about the barriers you may come across and excuses you may give yourself for not progressing towards your dream of running a successful cake business, and I will help you see those barriers for what they are, navigable!

I have encountered many barriers in my vision for success, in my own cake business and latterly in teaching in the cake industry and I have no doubt I will come across a few more but I look at them as hurdles to jump over, find the end and go around, or just roll my sleeves up and dig under. Or just burn the buggers out of existence.

I can now feel you thinking when is she going to get on about how I run a cake business.

Well the answer is without you controlling your mind with your goal clearly outlined and visualised daily, running a successful cake business could be a more difficult journey.I truly want you to be a successful cake business owner and I will use all the tried and tested techniques I know to get you there.

Some might have put the label at the start of this chapter describing the chapter as 'controlling your mind set', but I am a plain talking person, a cake maker and I don't fluff stuff up and I will only give you the tools you need, and the benefit of my experience to achieve your goal of running a successful cake business, and not fancy labels.

I find these new labels for things like 'mind set' are off-putting, and in themselves barriers to actually doing what is needed to be successful in your cake business.

So finally the last main ingredient.

4.   Learn Daily

Well, you have taken the first step on your learning journey to cake business success by purchasing this book. Now you must be open to a path of continuous learning on your journey.

I will cover all the important areas I feel and know will help you to succeed in the cake business later in the book as part of your learning.

You can also learn by allowing yourself development time in your week, 'protected learning time' I call it.

Perhaps instead of scrolling through endless Facebook posts of people's cats in hats, or 'hey look I'm on a beach' posts, use that time to learn. Replace that endless Facebook scrolling with perhaps a video teaching you a new cake technique or social media marketing tip.

It may be half an hour or more if you can spare it. Maybe on the train, or bus to work, or whilst eating your lunch, but make sure you aren't multitasking too much.

Note though, if you're with the kids, you're with the kids and that time is precious I feel, and not a time to learn. I am a big believer in being present.

Present with your kids or loved ones when you are with them, and showing up and being present in your cake business when you have scheduled to be. I suggest never mixing the two, if at all possible, as it leads to resentment and stress.

As far as learning is concerned, there is a wealth of information available on your phone, and on videos in areas you may feel you want to research to assist you in running a successful cake business. It may even be worth writing a learning plan. A simple one like 'I will learn a new cake technique a month '

Don't let your planning be overwhelming though, plan it out but tick it off as you do it. Now I can hear you thinking what the h**l Well, I am talking about you running a successful cake business, so we are going to tackle this like professionals and consider creating learning plans, or even just a list, but make yourself accountable for your own learning in your cake business.

You may have already undertaken learning in certain areas, like a business course or a marketing course, but things are continually evolving, believe me, and subjects such as marketing both online (social media) and offline (newspapers, ads & leaflets) change and evolve frequently.

So I have outlined the four main ingredients, above, but just to finish off this section I believe there are 5 other factors you need to bake your cake business success cake.

They are your mind set, your passion, your vision, your belief in yourself, and action! (I equate these five factors to conditions like correct oven temperature and freshness of ingredients etc.)

Without these other 5 extra factors, your ingredients are useless, and your success cake will not rise.

So look at your goal and vision board daily, but if you are not asking yourself daily "what have I done today to work towards my goal?" and "what can I do tomorrow to achieve my goal?" They will just be dreams.

So take action and let's go get you a successful cake business.

Let's Deliver Your Successful Cake Business

So you maybe still a bit puzzled by the methods I use to help you achieve success in the cake business, so I will tell you a little bit about me to help you understand how I can help you achieve your goal of running a successful cake business.

If you are making good money from your cakes, but working 60 hours a week to achieve this, then not only is this not sustainable for your health or your sanity, it is also not good for relations with friends and family.

(As I have said before if you work it out, you are possibly paying yourself well below the minimum wage and would be better off finding another job and keeping your cake making as a hobby.)

If you haven't launched your cake business yet be warned, the 60 hour a week model of working in the cake business is unsustainable and hopefully, after reading this book you will understand why you will never reach your cake business success by working at such a rate.

It does break my heart to hear the stories of highly skilled hard working cake makers working their socks off and being taken advantage of. I want to help and hopefully, you will let me and take on board what I have to say in this book.

This book is about creating a business that pays you your worth for your cakes, it's about getting more for less, working less for more.

More in terms of happiness, fulfilment, time to spend with loved ones and the money to help you do this. This book is about achieving your vision of running a successful cake business.

Less as in terms of the hours of your time away from the life you wish to lead with your family, less as in terms of stress, but not less in terms of quality of your cakes though.

But first if you are 'a pile it high, sell it cheap cake person 'then you may find the transformation to successful cake business owner a challenge, but not impossible. I do not advocate this as a cake business strategy.

I'm not a cake business coach who focuses on making 'a profitable cake business' or' making money from Cakes' as your number one focus, as I explained earlier I don't see this mind set as leading to success.

I have studied the psychology of successful people and as I said before, to focus on money is focusing on a negative, trust me on this one.

I am a businesswoman, a creator, and designer of fabulous cakes, and so are you. (Or a businessman)

So shoulders back and let's get this cake business the success it deserves

If you bought this book expecting me to be talking about baking with my grandma, and my mom, for years, I can do that, but I'm not soft and fluffy, I'm a businesswoman so don't expect soft and squishy reflections in this book.

So a bit about me so you can maybe see where I am coming from.

About me

I am a business coach and mentor and I specialise in helping men and women to start or grow a successful cake business. I have a certificate in teaching and coaching too.

I have been running a cake business for the past 20 years, only slowing it down when together with my business partner Jo, we set up The Cake Decorating Academy Specialising in teaching all levels of cake decorating 6 years ago.

I had been teaching cake decorating at University College Birmingham, (formerly The Birmingham College of Food), and had seen the need to provide modular one-day classes for adults in the West Midlands.

I concentrate now on making off cake commissions, and I teach bespoke private tuitions on a one to one basis when I am not coaching my cake business students, my Cakepreneurs, on how to start or run a successful cake business.

I suffer from Myalgic Encephalomyelitis (ME) after being diagnosed in 2007, and this has caused havoc with my cake decorating career, as I find it difficult to move, or use my hands on certain days, and my fatigue levels limit my working hours, as it is an illness that needs managing. But it's manageable with planning.

That's all I want to say about my illness. I don't wear it as a badge, and most of my students are unaware of it as I manage it as well as I can, although it meant that I had to step down from running my full-time cake business, as I couldn't manage my fatigue around my cake orders.

Now I wasn't successful straight away in my cake business. It was a long journey as I evolved and learned.

My learning was not in the how to achieve the best cake etc., as that was the easy part in my mind, no my learning and the key to my success was thinking and acting like a business woman!

Learning how to be a good business woman took it's time too, but as you will see in from this book, I now know the secret to being successful, and one of those secrets is thinking like a successful cake business owner from day one.

I have now taken this learning and I have been passing on the benefits of my experience, as well as the mistakes I made, helping to develop already established cake business owners, my Cakepreneurs, and would be cake business owners, to success in their own cake business.

So how did I start my cake journey?

Well, as I said before, I needed to earn more money. I became a single parent to two small babies, whilst working full time as a police officer. Money was tighter than tight, as I had to pay a mortgage, all the bills as well as child care, so we were on a tight budget.

The need to earn more money was not a good goal and I should have focused on a positive goal right from the start, but this was the very early days and I didn't know what I know now.

I loved baking and cake decorating, but we lived in an area where as my children grew up they were invited to very lavish parties, with the most amazing birthday cakes.

It soon became clear that my 'Sid the Snake' birthday cake from the local supermarket was not going to cut it with the 'playground moms' for very long.

So in preparation for when it was my turn to host a birthday party, I decided to take myself off and do a few cake decorating courses at The Birmingham College of Food. There wasn't any YouTube or the variety of magazines or online cake decorating courses that there are about these days.

As you may have guessed I'm no spring chicken, but, just like a well-fed fruit cake, I get better as I mature!

So to cut a long story short my birthday cakes were such a hit, with the playground moms, that they actually started ordering their celebration cakes from me!

Unfortunately, I fell into the trap, that scary zone of not knowing how to price my cakes correctly, and more importantly I didn't charge enough for the long hours it took me to produce those cakes.

I soon became disillusioned and burnt out believe me. I didn't have a sustainable cake business, I was playing at it.

My professional career then took me into areas that helped me take stock of what was going wrong in my own cake business.

My ME, meant that I went to work in the performance management department of the police force where I learned so much about running a business. I then used these strategies in my own cake business. (The Police Force is actually one big business which runs on budgets and targets.)

I was developing myself as a business woman, a business woman whose product was cake.

I then met my beautiful business partner, fabulous cake designer, and best friend Jo. We saw a gap in the market for one day short attended classes and cake decorating and Buttercream & Bows Cake Decorating Academy based in the Midlands in England was born.

Jo and I were qualified trainers and we developed our cake decorating classes, with lesson plans along the same lines of those taught academically at college, but with the emphasis on fun and enjoyment at the heart of every class.

Whilst teaching cake decorating it soon became apparent that a number of our cake decorating students wanted to start their own cake businesses and were asking me for advice.

I, therefore, put all my learning together, my business skills, my training and coaching qualifications, my psychology of success learning and knowledge of the cake business' and I began running one day attended classes in, 'starting a successful cake business' which I have been running for the last 7 years in the Midlands.

I then added to this with my Cakepreneur programme, coaching other cake business owners how to make a success of their cake businesses.

I can proudly name the students who have been on my cake business classes and who are now running successful cake businesses.

But they will tell you that from the start I ask them "Are you up for this challenge?"

They need to be willing to put my methods into practice, and so do you, because having a dream and actually working on the journey to cake business success are two different things.

I keep myself up to date and accountable in my business by using my coaches to keep me on track. Every successful business person has a coach or coaches, and so do I. My coach has her coach, and so on.

If you want success in the cake business you may need to get this support, and don't be afraid to ask for support from a coach.

Make sure that the business coach, if you choose to work with one, is the right fit for you, and you for them. This is the advice I give cake businesses owners from all over the world.

(If you want free advice about using a coach to guide you to cake business success, I am available to have a quick chat, I call it a 'discovery call' and you can book it via my website. I don't bite and no question is a stupid one either, I hope I can help you.)

What you need to understand though is this book, and others like it, are what I call shelf help.

In themselves, they can give you the blueprint for achieving your cake business success, but unless you are working on your mind set every day, the likelihood is you may not achieve your cake business success.

Make a plan and be accountable for that plan and take action every day to achieve your goal of running a successful cake business.

But it's a Saturated Market Place

So let's dispel the myth that the cake business is a saturated market.

This misconception is a barrier to your success in itself, and one of the reasons holding people back from starting or running a successful cake business.

I can remember being asked quite regularly to have a free display and demo stand for our cake decorating Academy in our local high-end department store, on their special review nights.

It was always a great evening, but I remember this one lady coming up to myself and Jo. She was in her late sixties perhaps, wearing a bright red coat and matching hat, and she said

" I tried running a cake business but everyone wanted my cakes for nothing, and no one will ever make any money running a cake business. There are too many people at it these days!"

I was surprised that she didn't have a black cloak with a hood and ringing a bell shouting

"We are all doomed!"

I remember smiling politely and offering her a slice of cake and a small shot of Baileys, which we always kept on the counter at the front, together with a couple of bowls of Quality Street.

(Nothing brings them up to the display quicker than a few brightly coloured sweets. We called these bowls our 'honey traps' as it always brought people over to us and created a buzz.)

Once the 'red devil' had stopped trying to suck all the enthusiasm I had for the cake business out of my body, I asked her if she had heard of Polly Porschen, Fiona Kearns, Mitch Turner, Lindy Smith, Eddie Spence (all my cake decorating business idols) to name but a few.

She hadn't and we carried on talking momentarily about cakes as I hadn't, and haven't got any time for naysayers and negative people, I tend to smile and avoid them.

They say surround yourself with successful people, and one of the reasons being is it is they who have the self-belief and confidence to achieve their success. They give off positivity and will not suck the life out of your enthusiasm.

With friends and family, who are naysayers, I don't tend to spend too much time around them, and if I can't avoid the interaction, I only discuss my business when asked directly "how it's going?"

My answer every time is "great!" I will never fuel their negative tank by discussing any business issues with them, as in my head and my heart I'm doing better than great.

So take a look in the area you have chosen to market and sell your beautiful cakes. Please note that I haven't said in your local area. I will explain in a later chapter that this may not be your ideal cake selling area or 'happy hunting ground' (HHG) as I call it.

Look at the cake business in that area. Travel to the heart of this territory, this 'happy hunting ground' and ask Google the question

'Cake decorators near me?' You may have to switch your phone on and off or allow location services in your settings to swop to this new area.

Make a list of the cake businesses in your 'happy hunting ground', and copy the links to their websites (if they have one). You will need them to do a competitor analysis which I will talk about later.

These other cake businesses may not be your competitors in that area in your happy hunting ground though!

The reason I am saying this is when it comes to the cake business I tend to think of the suppliers of beautiful cakes, cake business owners, such as yourselves, in a rather simplistic way.

An iceberg.

Imagine a triangle shaped iceberg, with the smaller tip of the iceberg above the waterline pointing up to the sky. Typical iceberg really. The rest, about 80 % of the iceberg, being below the water line.

Well for me the 80 % of the iceberg below the waterline represents most of your cake competitors in your chosen selling area, your 'happy hunting ground'. Harsh I know!

I am an 'all or nothing' person, 'go hard or go home' cake business coach, so I hope you are still with me here.

Carrying on...

The top 20% of the iceberg represents the top cake decorating businesses in your chosen selling area. The successful ones.

This 20 % is an absolute maximum though, from my research and it may be as low as 1%.

Therefore the 'Red Devil' I met pedaling her doom and gloom was mistaken. It is not a saturated market for those at the top of their game in the cake business, and it is not hard to stand out and join them.

Don't worry if there is a successful cake business in your happy hunting ground already. He or she will undoubtedly have their own cake style and brand, and you can trade successfully alongside them with your own distinct cake brand and style.

We will talk about 'real' cake business competition later in the book, but I will say it is healthy to have competition, as it focuses you, your brand and your cake business.

By reading this book you are aiming to be in the top percentage of cake business in your chosen area, in that section above the water. It is achievable.

I do not want you to spend any time in the larger section of the iceberg, the 80%, below the waterline, with those cake businesses that maybe haven't got a goal, and a vision for their cake business, and are just plodding along making cakes, and not being paid their worth.

You are a business owner and your cakes are high end. If you think you have gaps in your cake decorating knowledge it's time to start learning and updating your skills.

On my monthly coaching calls with my Cakepreneurs, I am still amazed when I get a sad face on the other end of the video call and the words

"There's another cake business started up around the corner!"

"Great," I say, "now go and introduce yourself and welcome them to the gang!"

Never look at another cake business opening up as a negative. It is usually one of the 80% of cake businesses that are 'under the water cake businesses' that are not going to challenge you for your spot above the water at the top of the iceberg.

If they are a professional cake business person they will welcome the professional friendship as you never know when you need a spare tin or you have forgotten to order the right extender for your cake box.

Having a real cake competitor is better as you can form an alliance and help each other if necessary.

You may have an enquiry for a cake order that you can't fit in, or it may not be the type of cake you would usually produce and vice versa.

I tended to pass on cake orders to other local cake businesses, to quote on, as I was purely focused towards the later years on the wedding cake market.

Be careful though that you know the standard of work of the other cake business, and that they are licensed etc.

Above all make sure you tell the enquirer that they may like to give this other person a call, but it is not a recommendation. Word it nicely. You wouldn't want to damage your reputation or brand by making a recommendation that came back to haunt you.

This sort of alliance has benefited me too in the past as the other cake business has passed orders on to me, when they are busy or it was outside of their cake portfolio.

I have even baked cakes and stored them for other businesses, and took on their delivery and set up for a wedding cake, or assisted with it. Never say never we are in it together is my motto. As long as I wasn't busy and was comfortable being associated with the other cake business I didn't see any harm.

I cannot say that I have ever met another local cake business owner who didn't see this mutual respect and collaboration at times as a win-win either.

If you do come across another cake business maybe give them this book, when you have finished.. only joking, you do not want to give them too much of an advantage!

I want you in all aspects of your cake business, or in the planning of one, to work smarter, not harder, and I will outline how this can be done if your dream is to run or grow a successful cake business

Cake Smash Your Barriers

So you have your goal of what running a successful cake business will bring you, and you can hopefully see it displayed on your fridge, alongside your vision board, and you can feel the smile on your face when you imagine living the life you want, as a result of running a successful cake business.

Now let's talk a little about the barriers you may face to you achieving your goal and your success.

The biggest barrier to your success is you, and your belief in yourself.

If you have the belief that you haven't got the skills to produce the cakes you need to produce, then go and get the skills, quick and easy. That's one self-limiting belief dealt with.

Learn from the internet, ask fellow cake makers and get help for free, or attend a class and or buy a magazine to help you.

Now you have your goal and your vision of what a successful cake business will bring you, you will need to take note of the other big barriers to your cake business success journey.

These count equally whether you are starting up a cake business, or have been running a cake business for a while.

Having coached many cake biz students, over the years, and I have identified the two biggest barriers most of them have faced initially when starting their cake business, after lack of self- belief, confidence, not having a goal and a vision.

Those barriers to success are family and friends!

Believe me, family and friends, without knowingly doing it, will put up those barriers to your success in the cake business for you. It's human nature to care for those close to us and to point out the dangers and potential pitfalls of setting up a new business, especially a cake business.

Family and friends will build those barriers to success, in your head, as if you gave them the nails and the materials to build them, and said go ahead build me those barriers to cake business success.

They may say things like

"You won't make enough money to pay the rent/mortgage" "You have never made a wedding cake before"

"There are too many people selling cakes"

"My Aunty used to do it, and she never made any money!"

Don't worry though, you can stop yourself from giving them the barrier making materials and access to your head. You can stop them from dragging down your ambitions, or from sabotaging your cake business success from the start.

Firstly you are now mindful of these potential barrier makers and you can try and prevent them from doing so by letting them know your goal and share your vision with them from the start, today, now......

Sit your nearest and dearest down and tell them, maybe with a plate of your delicious cake in front of them, " I am going to run a successful cake business", and that you would like them to go on that journey to cake business success with you.

Like a road trip, but that you are the driver and they are the support team on your cake success bus.

Pick a good time to make this announcement, maybe over a coffee, face to face, or over a meal. Don't just walk into the lounge, whilst the TV is on, and challenge for your nearest and dearest attention.

Treat this announcement like you are the Prime Minister making a short announcement in the street outside 10 Downing Street to awaiting news cameras and photographers. Give your nearest and dearest the headlines, and tell them the details, the plan will follow.

It is important that you take this seriously, and pick your time and place.

You are selling them your vision, and maybe asking them to join you on your journey to cake business success, or not as the case may be!

You may want to wait a while before you do this, it's entirely up to you, as you may be the type of person who needs to have your cake business success plan mapped out in order to answer those tricky questions.

Entirely up to you.

Let family and friends offer to help and try and involve them in your journey to cake business success. They may have social media, or web skills, or useful contacts, but do not let them drive your cake success bus, you are the driver, and the project manager of this road trip to a successful cake business.

Don't get me wrong, you would love to hear their ideas or a direction for your cake business, but it's your journey, you have the map and are therefore are the most informed. It's you that will carry out the learning required and reading this book, although you can suggest they read it with you.

I began to coach a lady in the early days of her cake business, who outlined her goal to me, of living in a slightly bigger house, with a more reliable car with her husband and four children. Her vision board showed a big modern shiny white kitchen with her making breakfast for everyone before they went off to school. This is what she wanted a successful cake business to deliver for her.

She was still working as a busy lawyer and had never taken the children to or collected them from school, and had missed every school play as she couldn't get the time off.

Her dream was to spend the summer holidays making cakes and taking her children out on trips, after ditching her day job and running her own successful cake business.

But she fell at one of the first barriers. She gave her husband the keys to the cake success bus and let him drive it. This may or may not be a bad thing for some of you, but for her it was.

Now I knew her husband, a lovely intelligent guy with his own retail business, and he had plenty of business skills he could share with his wife to make her cake business a success. He was fully on board with his wife's goal and vision to slowly decrease her hours as a lawyer and eventually run her own successful cake business full time.

But she gave him the keys to the cake success bus and he took over the driving seat and they nearly ended up coming off the road and ending up in the cheap cakey ditch.

Now cheap cakey ditch is in the middle of cheap cakey town, where the cake business people who live there work too many hours, and don't spend any quality time with their nearest and dearest. They work for less than the minimum wage and have booked their place in its very own Burn Out Hotel.

How did she give her husband the keys to her success bus? Well, she let her husband decide that his wife was going to be the best competitive cake business owner is her area. He took her down the 'sell lots of cake at the cheapest price in the area' route.

He had lots of contacts who wanted cakes at the best price and thought she would make a killing in her cake business. Well, it nearly killed her and their marriage as she burnt out quite quickly!

She was working well below the minimum wage, working all hours and spending little time with her loved ones. She wasn't living her idea of success which was to spend more time with her children and make an income to replace her previous lawyer's wage and the signs were she would never achieve this income goal as she was exhausted.

Now his strategy was a good one for her husband's retail business, but it wasn't the right one for his wife to build a successful cake business.

Giving her husband the driving seat was due to lack of self-belief and confidence in herself, and doing what we always do, we go and give the 'difficult bits' to the so-called experts instead of trusting ourselves.

I say use the 'experts' in your cake business but do not ask them to drive, remember they are your technical support on the cake success bus but you are in the driving seat.

So stay in control of the cake business success bus.

It may be the case that your nearest and dearest is getting a bit above themselves, in their technical support role in your cake business, at the time of reading this book. Don't worry though you can stop your bus and put yourself back on course.

I helped my Cakepreneur lawyer student to do this. It didn't take much for her to rethink her cake business and relaunch. She is well on the way to achieving her Goal and Vision now, she is still married, and she is spending lots of quality time with her children which were part of her goal and her vision of what success in the cake business meant for her.

So there may be other barriers to success popping into your head at the moment like:

"I can't charge what I need and deserve for my cakes in my area"

"I haven't got enough time to start a business with working full time"

Well, don't worry we will be smashing down these barriers to cake business success in the following chapters so see you there.

Chapter 2 You're in business

Think Like a Business Owner

At the start of my attended cake business classes, straight after 'goal and vision' setting and encouraging your nearest and dearest to come on the journey to a successful cake business with you, I always jumped straight into the section which I called my 'Louis Walsh' section.

(Louis Walsh is an Irish TV personality who has a saying 'you look like a popstar, you sound like a pop star, you are a pop star!)

Well, guess what, I want you to look like a business woman/ man, I want you to sound like a businesswoman/man and behold you are a business woman/ man!

You're a business owner, and your business is cake!

It isn't hard to get ahead if you look and sound the part.

Before you go out and buy an expensive suit, and or a briefcase, let's explore what I mean.

Take a look on the internet at some of the top 50 cake businesses and their respective owners. See how they present themselves. Look at the lovely Mitch Turner and Peggy Porschen to name but a few. (Male cake business owners are in the top 50 too!)

Most will be in chefs whites photographed with their cakes. Always a good shot. Also pay attention to their brand colours, on their websites and social media. You may see their brand colours reflected in their outfits on their official pictures. (We will cover branding in chapter 4, in more detail, so don't worry)

I am not saying dress in your brand colours every day when meeting potential cake customers, which is impractical. No, what I am saying is that, as the owner of a food business, a cake business, clean hair, clean nails, and clothes are a must. If your nails are painted, make sure they aren't chipped or cracked. I'm not going to nanny anyone here, but you get my train of thought.

That goes for your car too. If your car is going to be visible to the potential cake customer make sure it's clean. First impressions and all that! I will let you into a secret here. Whenever I go to eat anywhere, be it a curry house, pizza shop, a top class restaurant I always pop to the loo first.

If it isn't clean, and I mean the sinks etc. too, I will not eat there. Okay, this is possibly just me, but first impressions count. If the restaurant can't be bothered with the hygiene of their toilets, how careful are they with their hygiene in their kitchen?

So look like a cake business owner. Clean smart casual at the least. I must admit I do have my 'meeting customer's outfits' which are a stable from years ago. They never go out of fashion, in fact, they may never have been in fashion, but this is about looking professional.

If you have a shop/cafe or stall where you sell your cakes, make sure you are ready to don your clean apron to speak to customers. It's the little things that put you above the rest and instils confidence in your cake customers.

Maybe invest in a branded T-shirt, with your telephone number printed largely on the rear.

So you are now looking like the owner of a successful cake business, now let's sound like one. It may be the edge the customer needs to seal that cake order.

Luckily 80% of your contact with potential cake customers will be via the telephone, or over the internet. No need to be 'on brand' when you are at the end of the telephone, or in front of your laptop, who hasn't got one of those office onesies!

I cannot stress how important it is to make every contact you have with a potential cake customer count.

Every contact counts!

Make the customer feel special during every contact they have with you.

If you can have a separate telephone for your business so that you can answer any call with "Good Morning / Afternoon The Successful Cake Company, how can I help you?"

Note that I didn't put Good Evening!

This is because success to most of us includes a good work-life balance, so that telephone may go onto answer phone in the evening. But please ensure you have a cheerful professional answer phone message greeting the customer and explaining

- Welcome to your cake company name
- Apologise for missing their call.
- Explain your opening or office hours.
- Ask them to leave a message or visit your website and fill in a contact form or simply text their enquiry and you will get back to them as soon as possible. Manage their expectations of a time frame i.e. 24hrs reply time.
- Finally, thank them for their call.

This may seem a bit basic, but you will be amazed at the lack of answer phone messages or information when you call a cake business and hear their answer phone.

Every contact counts remember. If you are too nervous to record the answer phone message yourself, then ask someone with a good telephone voice to do it for you.

Now it is the 21st Century, and there are so many different ways of contacting your cake business from Facebook messenger through to Instagram messages etc.

Just remember we are a professional cake business and the professional approach outlined above needs to be carried through across all our outward facing forms of contact.

(It might be worth mentioning here that the more social media platforms you are on the more time you will spend finding the messages and answering them.

It may be worth managing your customer's expectations of your cake business by posting the details of how to contact you. Try and make it one channel. Your website, telephone or Facebook messenger perhaps.)

If your business contact number is a mobile telephone, make sure the 'WhatsApp' picture associated with this mobile telephone number is either your logo or one of your show stopping cakes. You dressed as Little Red Riding Hood just won't cut a professional image. I must admit I was guilty of that one in the early days of 'WhatsApp' as I never expected a customer to contact me via this ... wrong!

If you are going to have a business Facebook page, which I think is a must, then ensure this corpocracy is carried across in the thumbnail pictures.

So now you are looking and sounding like a successful cake business owner, so let's now consider your written approach.

Emails are another very popular way of contacting you, and if you have a website, you will hopefully have a 'contact us' form.

I do strongly suggest that you obtain a professional email associated with your website rather than the very popular Gmail accounts.

If your website is www.prettybuttercupsbakery then you could have diana@prettybuttercupsbakery, or info@prettybuttercupsbakery as your email address.

Having a professional email address is helpful when using email marketing platforms such as 'Mail Chimp'. Marketing emails from some Gmail accounts can end up in the cake customers spam folders.

Gathering email contact names can be very useful as straight away you have an email address to add to your marketing list.

Always ensure you have a business sign off at the end of your cake business email too. You can do this by going to your email settings and formulating your closing signature. This is what I suggest you include at the end of every email.

- Thank you for your email and I look forward to hearing from you again.
- Maybe include a handwritten signature
- Include your telephone number
- Always include a request to visit and a link to your website, Facebook page, and any other social media site.
- If you are a Limited Company you have to include your corporation number.

Finally, put an out of office reply onto your email on permanently.

This is so useful for when you are busily creating wonderful cakes, meeting with cake customers, enjoying quality time with your family, or if you are just starting out you may be busy with your day job.

This out of office, bounce back email should contain all the same information you recorded on your answer phone message. This makes your customers feel secure that they will be contacted as soon as possible, or within a given time frame. Make sure you do reply within that time frame though.

Try and streamline the admin for your cake business from day one. Save yourself lots of valuable time and you will be running your cake business and it won't be running you.

If your cake business 'operating budget' allows, and certainly as you get busier, you may like to consider a telephone answering service.

Most telephone answering services are fairly cheap, and you can usually gain a trial period to try out the service. Maybe get a few mystery customers to call regarding cake orders on your behalf to test the service out.

Another consideration, as you get busier, to free you up to carry on developing your successful cake business, or to enjoy a better work-life balance, is hiring the services of a Virtual Assistant to carry out many of those cake business admin functions.

Now, this might be a suggestion too far at this stage, as you hurl this book across the room.

Well bear with me please and read on, as I want you to be the best you can be and reach and see the success you can achieve in the cake business.

These delegated services may not be for you right now but consider them later perhaps as you cannot do everything as your cake business grows.

The key to any successful business is working 80% on your business and 20% in your business!

For you, this may mean being the designer, the creator behind your fabulous cakes, but not carrying out all the tasks needed to run the business. Free to create and bake when you want but not driven by necessity to carry out these functions.

You can now see that being a successful cake business owner is akin to one of those old- fashioned buskers outside of a tube station playing the guitar, a harmonica and banging a drum on their back at the same time.

So now is the time to sit down and plan in when you are going to start delegating some of those cake business tasks before you become overwhelmed and you risk burn out and your customers feeling frustrated or going elsewhere.

I do recommend outsourcing functions such as admin and social media right from the start.

You are after all a cake designer, maker and decorator, and sometimes when time is money we must play to our strengths and outsource other business functions, in order to be successful.

What Type of Business Are You?

So now you are looking and sounding like a successful cake business owner, it's time to check out what type of cake business you are, or are planning to be. Are you the right sort of business?

Again I shudder as this brings back memories of years ago when I thought I would start out on the right foot and open a business bank account.

I turned up on a Saturday morning, at a well-known high street bank, and sat down in front of the business banking manager full of excitement. This didn't last long as the first question that came out of his mouth was

"So what type of business are you then?"

My reply "I'm a cake business! "Just didn't seem to be the right answer, and I felt about two inches tall and a bit of an idiot.

"Are you a sole trader, a partnership or a limited company? " He asked.

Well, I hadn't a clue, so I felt a must to include a little bit about this in the book. Hopefully, you are fully aware of the differences and legalities surrounding them.

I won't be going into depth about this very dry subject as there is a great deal of information is available, on the internet, written by people far more qualified than I am on the subject. But what I will aim to do is highlight a few things you may not know.

(Can I remind you that this Cake Biz Success book refers to the United Kingdom in 2018 and is correct at the time of going to print)

So what are the different types of business?

Sole Trader - The simplest kind of business and most cake businesses are sole traders. As a sole trader, you are personally responsible for the money your cake business owes.

A gentle word of warning. If you are in receipt of any type of benefit you will need to give the Department of Work and Pensions, DWP, a call to check if your new income will affect your benefit. Again you can find them on the internet at www.gov.uk.

Partnerships - are two or more people jointly running a cake business, and, like a sole trader, both are liable for any money owing in the cake businesses name.

(There is also the limited liability partnership (LLP) option, which is common amongst other professionals, where 2 or more people set up a cake business and they are responsible for paying their own taxes, but they are not personally responsible for any debts the cake business can't pay.)

It is a big must that with any partnership, even a husband and wife team, relatives or otherwise, acting as sole traders or a limited company, that all parties take legal advice and get a 'Partnership Agreement' written for their cake business.

No one can predict the future, and it protects all involved. You do not have to get this legally drawn up, but I strongly advise this.

Limited Company - This is sometimes a bit more complicated to set up, but it keeps your cake business separate from your personal assets. You may find it useful to get the help of a solicitor, or an accountant to help you form a limited company, but you can set it up yourself, online, it isn't that difficult, and the fee is very small. Be careful when filling out the forms though as they form a legal document and therefore all the information must be correct.

It can be more expensive to complete your cake business accounts as a limited company, as they are usually completed by an accountant, and that is more expensive than doing your accounts yourself.

Also if you do not file your accounts with Companies House, there is a penalty to pay .In addition, company directors can be prosecuted and disqualified from being a company director or taking part in the management of a company for five years. So best seek professional advice.

Your information such as your name and address are in the public domain as a company director of a limited company. This can be avoided if you use a 'formation company' who will, for a fee, provide a registered office, service and business address. Ask your solicitor or accountant as they might offer the same service too.

I personally cannot see a reason to hide who you are in public as your customers invariably know where you live if they are collecting cakes from you. (It does put your age out there in public though, so no more knocking off a few years if you are single.)

Also with limited companies, there isn't the freedom that you get with other types of business with naming your cake business.

If the name you want is already registered you cannot register a limited company with the same name in the UK.

Another consideration, with a limited company, is that you are a shareholder. As a shareholder, if something were to happen to you, you may need a will to reflect the fact that you are a shareholder of a limited company. Again you will need legal guidance on this.

That said, I am the Director of a limited company even considering the drawbacks.

Once again I cannot guide you as to what type of Cake Company you might like to form, I can only advise you to take professional advice.

If you look at the Companies House web page there's lots more information on there. You will find Companies House at www.gov.uk.

Please note that with any form of cake business, whether it be a sole trader, a limited company, or a partnership, that you, or anyone else working in your cake business, must register with HMRC online in order to pay your tax and national insurance. Also as a self-employed person, you will need to complete a tax return!

Tax returns are changing soon too. It doesn't matter what type of Cake Company you are, you will be required to submit your tax return quarterly. Frightening thought!

The rules regarding registering with HMRC and exactly when to do it are on their website.www.gov.uk

Now that what type of cake business you want to be, or are, is a bit clearer in your mind, let's just revisit where we are.

You are now hopefully looking more like a professional cake business owner, and you have sorted your emails/ answer phone messages etc. so that you are sounding like the one too.

I will talk later about cake customer consultations and quotes, from holding a wedding cake consultation to confidently informing your customers of the cost of their cake, face to face, or more commonly over the telephone.

So let's revisit, for the final time, the bit where you sound like the professional cake business owner that you are, now that you have it clear in your mind as to what type of company your cake business is, or will be.

You now own a company or are a company director! So keep telling yourself this!

Next, you need to tell others!

This was a major stumbling block for me when I started my cake business.

I had been running my own cake business for a while, but I wanted to branch out from celebration and cupcakes, into the wedding cake market, which I found was more profitable for me and gave me the best return on my time. Don't forget my motto is work smarter not harder!

I had a goal, I had a vision, I had a plan of being a success in the cake business, but it didn't seem to be working.

I looked at everything, and then something that had bothered me for a while woke me up one night, and I realised what the problem was.

The issue was that when I saw all friends and colleagues, they would say, "Hi, how are you doing, are you still doing your cupcakes?" Or "Here is the cupcake lady!"

What's wrong with that you may ask? Well nothing, but I was so much more than a "cupcake lady".

(I wanted to be Mitch Turner or the next Peggy Porschen, my idols.)

I was a professional sugar craft artist, I had made my own bespoke range of wedding cakes. I was teaching cake decorating at a high level at University, and I wanted to be recognised for the skilled professional that I had become.

The issue was, I was this person inside the tin, so to speak, but it didn't say that on the outside of the tin!

Then it came to me, whilst really looking into branding and marketing, and speaking to my business coach.

What I came to realise, I suppose, does come under the heading of branding, which we will cover in more depth in chapter 4, as branding is much more than a logo and colours. We are our cake brand!

We brand ourselves in everything we do and say.

The image and impression of my cake brand, I was giving out on, social media and on my web website, said 'middle of the road cakey lady'. Nowt wrong with that but I wanted much more for my cake business.

The image and branding that I was actually displaying said I was the owner of a cake business, together with those cake business owners lumped into the 80% of the iceberg, below the waterline, which I described in Chapter 1. I was in a saturated market, crowded market.

I thought I looked like a business woman, but I wasn't necessarily talking like a business woman, in all my communications with the outside world. My Facebook, website, everything.

So I changed my tactics. Whenever I met old friends or colleagues, at a social event, meeting or even at the supermarket, I told them exactly what I was doing, if asked.

This is where I needed to set my stall out and manage everybody's expectations of me.

I told them I was a company director and I supplied handcrafted bespoke couture wedding cakes.

Or I if I didn't know them, I said

"Hi I'm Diana, and I have my own company"

"I'm a bespoke sugar craft artist specialising in bespoke wedding cakes."

Let's break this down. I am extremely confident and proficient in sugar craft, and so hopefully are you, unless you specialise in a niche area like macarons or chocolate, and your skills can be described in another way.

Don't worry if you aren't confident or proficient at the moment, as you can quickly learn these skills so that you can refer to yourself in this way, once you have.

Bespoke, well let's face it everyone that comes to us to make them a cake, have in their mind a picture they have seen on Pinterest, a bespoke design usually. They are actually commissioning us to design and make their cake. Or you may have a portfolio of cakes that you have developed and designed, which are bespoke designs to you.

Quick warning here! Be very careful if your customer shows you a picture of a cake from the internet, it will more than likely be someone else's design, and you have no right to replicate this cake without the permission of the other cake business owner.

So the lesson I learned was to let others know you are a professional and a business owner, and your product is cake!

Keep An Eye On The Profits – Book Keeping and Accounting

How do you know you are making a success of your cake business?

Well, I'm sorry to say this but bookkeeping is the only way to measure your success and to keep you on target. Keeping track of your expenses and income is the key to a successful cake business. Simples.

This is the part of a business that every cake business owner hates, and I'm included in this. But it is the backbone of your business and the key to your cake business success, believe me.

Bookkeeping is a non-negotiable part of running a successful cake business, so take a deep breath and look at your vision board, you know the one where you outlined your dream of your successful life and what it looks like, the one you are going to work hard for by running a successful cake business.

Your vision board should be on the front of your phone as a screen saver or pinned to the front of your fridge. Go and re-read chapter 1 if you need the enthusiasm for bookkeeping.

Sorry to Laura and Rick, my accountants, but it is my least popular task.

I soon saw the benefit to me as a cake business professional of keeping my version of my 'books'. It clearly showed to me that I was on target to meet my goals, or not as the case may be, and would be the barometer for measuring my cake business success.

My books, however, crude would show me that I was running my business in budget, making a real wage, and keeping up to my profit margin target. (Yes profit margin target, we will discuss this in chapter 5 - Pricing, but bear with me)

It showed me that I was on target to achieve my goal.

When it didn't I just sat down and looked at what I was doing wrong, had a word with myself and analysed where I was going off course.

I mentor and coach many cake business owners to achieve success in their cake businesses, and failure to set targets and monitor them by keeping books is one of the reasons they veer off course.

Don't get me wrong, I did spend too many years just taking the money and trying to tot it up as I went along, and I got into a right mess, possibly working for less than the minimum wage, which there wasn't one in those days.

I will never know as my bookkeeping was practically non-existent in the old days. I did pay my tax and National Insurance though, but I possibly paid over the odds for fear of not getting it right.

I didn't claim for half the things I should have claimed for as a business expense against tax, such as my telephone, mileage, allowance for my using my kitchen and my office at home, the list goes on. I didn't even claim for my printer ink or the paper I printed my leaflets on, in a way I was treating my business as a hobby.

Now you can glaze over at this point and ignore my advice, but the success of your business starts and ends with your bookkeeping.

But there is, however, a silver lining, you can outsource this admin function of your cake business, to a professional or someone that just loves keeping your books.

My top tip is to hand this over to a professional or someone else as soon as you can and add the cost of this bookkeeping to your operating costs.

I did go on a free business class with the bank. It was okay, but not the best and I read books, but no one appeared to understand us cake makers and our unusual business.

Even if you just keep two excel spreadsheets with 'Money In' and the other with 'Money Out' each month, this will be better than nothing.

Make sure you keep receipts and invoices for purchases. That receipt showing a pack of butter from Sainsbury's, with all your other personal purchases on is still a business receipt and needs to be kept just in case HMRC wants to see it.

The simplest way is to have an envelope for each month to put your receipts in, or you could download an app like QuickBooks, where you take a photograph of your receipt and attach it to your 'Money Out' file on the app.

When Jo and I formed our Buttercream and Bows, the business advisor we spoke too introduced us to an accountant. Both the business advisor and the accountant were as useful as chocolate teapots, but that is a whole other story. What I am trying to say is be very careful who you do get to advise you, as not everyone is the right fit so to speak.

Legally if you are an LLP or Ltd cake business, under UK Law, you are required to keep books and have them completed by an authorized accountant.

Well, this first accountant did his job, talked in a business language that we didn't understand and wasn't the best fit for us at all.

Then we had a chance meeting with Rick, our current accountant, at a networking meeting, and then we met the fabulous Laura our other accountant from Smart Online Accountants.

What a breath of fresh air they were. They talked our language, and we grew as business women as a result of their free advice and guidance.

They were a critical part of our business. The right fit for us.

Check out Laura's really helpful website at www.smartonlineaccounts.co.uk

Stick to what you know best is my motto. If a task will take you hours or years to learn then consider not wasting your time. Pay to take the shortcut and outsource your bookkeeping.

There's a simple way to keep track of your money using a sheet of paper with two columns. Incomings and Outgoings. Not the best as you need to keep an eye on the actual cash flow, but it is a start.

Next, there is an excel spreadsheet with these two columns on it, which with a bit of magic adds it up for you as you go along. A sheet for each month. You could build in other functions on this spreadsheet to give you cash flow if you have the skills which I don't have.

The final option and the best one I think is what I do. I send all my bank statements and receipts in a prepaid envelope or online to Laura at Smart Online Accountants each month, and for a very small fee, equivalent to a Costa coffee a day, or less she does my books for me.

Right, so some more basics. If you are a sole trader you are not legally required in the UK to have a business bank account. As an Ltd company, you are.

But although you don't need a business bank account as a sole trader, banks are now putting clauses into their personal bank accounts stating that they are not to be used for business purposes.

I highly recommend though that you do have a separate bank business bank account for your cake business as a sole trader, as it makes bookkeeping far simpler.

I also recommend a second or separate bank account where you can regularly drop your tax and National Insurance contributions into, to keep you from spending it.

You may also want to set up a third party payment provider attached to your bank account so that you can accept card payments online or over the phone. The best-known one is PayPal but you will need to set up a merchant account, not a private individual account with them.

There are many other third-party payment platforms with varying fees for processing payments. Typically they take 2.3 - 3.0 % commission.

I cannot recommend to you enough that you set one of these third-party payment systems up as cheques are a thing of the past really and so is cash increasingly.

(If someone wants to pay you by cheque then it is you that has to drive down to the bank, park and put that cheque in the bank. That's time and effort out of your day where you could be working on or in your cake business or with your loved ones enjoying leisure time.)

I remember a few years back at a large craft fair where Jo and I sold our cake decorating classes and gift vouchers for experience days.

I saw other stall holders losing out on sales as no one carries cash anymore.

Fortunately for us, we took the step early on in our business to use PayPal which I had attached to my iPhone, and we were able to make sales there and then at the craft market.

Since then many others payment platforms that can attach to your smartphone have come along, but it was a blessing at the time to our business to be able to use our mobile phones to take payments and deposits whilst being out and about.

This is so useful to your cake business as you can take full payment or deposits over the telephone or send an invoice link in an email.

Hobby Caker to Successful Business Owner

Why start a cake business when there are lots of others doing it already?

Well, imagine what Richard Branson thought when he started Virgin Airlines. The market was already saturated with the big boys and girls (British Airways etc.) appearing to have it all sewn up. But that didn't stop him as he saw an opening.

Richard Branson saw that there was an opening to do things differently, with a strong brand and identity and he focused heavily on delivering good customer service.

There are big openings too and opportunities at the top end of the cake selling market that can be filled by you and your cake business.

With careful planning and focus you won't have that much competition as there are lots who are playing at running a cake business, and not making much money out of it believe me. I was one of them!

Now playing at it is not meant in any derogatory way as there are lots of hobby cakers out there enjoying what they are doing, and I do not have any issue with them. Making cakes is their hobby and long may they enjoy that it and gain pleasure from it.

Take a walk around the food halls in your big stores, or the local supermarket and look at the cakes they have on offer. Mass manufactured basic designs. It makes you want to scream, or is it just me!

(My Sid the Snake cake seems to have disappeared off the shelves though these days)

The cakes our beginner cake decorating students walked out with, having attended our 'Cup Cake Master' or' Introduction to Cake Decorating Class' at our Cake Decorating Academy were streets ahead in terms of quality. It is very easy to shine believe me.

These mass-produced celebration cakes are fine for the customer who isn't too bothered about quality or originality, but that is not the customer we are courting.

There is a demographic of cake customer out there that wants a bespoke design, crafted by a professional cake maker who offers quality customer service and values it's customers.

I remember at Christmas time dashing into a supermarket to grab some last minute mince pies as I remembered a lady I was meeting was a vegetarian.

(Yes I do buy mince pies from the supermarket as they are far better and quicker than mine.)

I asked the assistant in the bakery aisle of the supermarket the location of the vegetarian mince pies.

He looked puzzled and quickly informed me that all their mince pies were vegetarian. Oops!!!

This is what will differentiate us as professional cake business owners from the stack them high, sell them cheap mentality of the supermarket.

Our ideal cake customer wants us to fully understand their needs and be able to accommodate their needs, seamlessly, and that's why our ideal customer won't be buying their celebration cakes from the local supermarket.

So if you are thinking about starting a cake business because you don't like that Monday morning feeling, or would like to take the kids to school and pick them up, and have a nutritious meal waiting for them, or you just want to get off that treadmill of early starts, traffic, and stress, by running a successful cake business, then start by planning your business now.

If you have been running your cake business for a while and think that you need to rethink a few things then carry on reading. There is no failure in business just lack of focus on your vision for your successful life.

I have fallen in every cake business owner's pothole I could ever end up in but I've learned and now I want to pass this on to you.

Going from a Hobby Caker to a Cake Business Owner

You may be a very keen hobby caker/cake decorator and you have bought or acquired lots of baking and cake decorating equipment and gadgets over the years.

Now, this may seem crazy, but how about laying them all out on the kitchen or dining room table. Go on every single bit if it. Tins, mixers, ice cream scoops (for filling cupcake cases) and of course the big-ticket items like your mixer.

These are the items you as a hobby caker are now going to sell to you the professional businessman or woman who has a cake business. When I say sell, I mean sell on paper so that you can claim the cost of these purchases against your tax.

What do I mean? Well, say it all came to £900. When you get to the end of the year that will be £900 you won't be paying in tax as you have an outgoing of £900 to allow for. Now there are rules like the 25% depreciation rule let me explain.

So you purchased your Kenwood mixer 2 years ago and it let's say £250, and you still have the receipt for it. Under the depreciation rule after the first year, the value is now £187.50.

So after 2 years, the £187.50 depreciates another 25%, so you the hobby caker can sell you the businessman/woman the mixer for £140.62.

Maths lesson over, but let's be clear you will only do this on big-ticket cake decorating equipment.

Don't forget that you the professional cake business owner needs other equipment to run a successful cake business.

A laptop or tablet, a printer, an oven. You can sell these to your business to observing the 25% rule.

Let's take a look at the oven for baking your cakes.

You need to work out is this an oven for the sole purpose of baking cakes, or will you be using it for you and the family to rustle up home-baked foods.

If the oven is needed for domestic too you need to work out what percentage of it is for your business and what percentage is for your domestic use.

For this example let's say it's 50/50.

So you purchased a new oven 1 year ago costing £500. You can only claim half of this cost, as its use is 50/50. Therefore under the depreciation rule, you can sell it to yourself one year later for £187.50.

Personally, I do not use my cake oven for family meals as it can cause a greasy layer to form when my son pops in his chicken nuggets etc. in the oven.

I keep the oven purely for baking cakes, and I purchased a halogen countertop oven quite a number of years ago and the family food is cooked it this. Yes, I cook a whole Sunday roast, the chicken and the roast veg in my halogen oven, and it grills a mean full English breakfast too.

This way I can claim the full cost of my big oven for my business against tax! Remember I said only do this on the big-ticket items or you will lose the will to bake!

So you will have produced a list of all the equipment and costs you need to now sell yourself. What do you do with it?

After adding the total cost up you can divide it up and add it to your operating costs per month or per hour (See pricing structures in chapter 5) or you can wait until the year-end, when your tax return is due and take this off the amount you the businessman/woman has earnt in your business, therefore paying less tax.

If you are in any doubt about what I have said please get independent financial advice as I'm not an accountant or tax adviser.

My final words on moving from this being your hobby to your full time profession is that you need to let those around you and those who have benefited from your hobby in the past know that you are now running a professional cake business. Thank them for their support in the past but now ask for their support in your professional business.

Don't forget we mentioned that friends and family, who supported you as a hobby caker can now be the hindrance or put up barriers to your progress so get them on board with the new cake business now.

Chapter 3 Finding Your Ideal Cake Customer

Why it's Important to Define Them

Hopefully, by now you are seeing the bigger picture, and starting to appreciate that your cake business is not open to everyone!

Damn right it isn't, as you aren't interested in the cheap cake hunters, who will waste your time and energy just trying to haggle with you. We don't do haggling; the price is the price for your hard work and professionalism. You seek the ideal cake customer.

You need to understand that your cake business has an ideal cake customer.

Now a good friend told me a story which I will shorten considerably. I am not certain of its origin, it isn't known, but I think it is important. It's not a cakey story, but it helps me prove my point.

A large cargo vessel broke down in the middle of the ocean and the engine could not be fixed by the skeleton staff of crew on board. A local fisherman was summoned, who it was said was an expert at fixing such engines, but it would cost 5,000 dollars for him to look at it.

Given no other solution, the Captain summoned the local fisherman to attend to the broke engine on board the vessel.

The local fisherman approached the stricken engine, took out an old wooden mallet from his bag, and hit the engine hard with a loud bang. The engine immediately started and the problem was fixed.

The Captain then challenged paying the fisherman the 5,000 dollars, saying that all the fisherman had done was hit the engine once with a hammer which cost no more than 1 dollar.

The fisherman replied that yes that was true that the equipment needed to fix the problem was inexpensive, yet the years and professional knowledge needed to know how to use the hammer and where exactly to hit the engine was what the captain was paying for.

Yes, the ingredients for your cakes may be inexpensive, but your time and skill is what the customer is paying for.

So you are a bespoke cake making service, and just like any other bespoke craftsperson, you will have your defined customer base, your ideal cake customer.

You are not a one size fits all cake business, as this is not a recipe for success.

To achieve cake business success, you need to know who are the right customers for your cake business, and who are the wrong customers, and you haven't got the time on your cake success journey to convert the wrong ones, so steer well clear.

One of my cake business coaching clients challenged me on this view, the other day. She asked that surely any customer is a good customer and money in the bank so to speak.

Well if you are looking for offenders in this category then I have been guilty of thinking like this in the past too, much to my own annoyance.

Then I did not have the benefit of my extensive learning in the art of success in business.

I was working till late at night, in my cake business, for very little money and neglecting my health, my family and my relationships with my 'any business is money in the bank strategy'.

In order to achieve success and realise your vision of a successful life delivered through running a successful cake business, you will to have a plan, a route map with a clear destination towards success ahead of you, and this includes finding your ideal cake customer.

By the end of chapter 5, you will have formulated your cake pricing strategy and that together with other elements will give you the clear direction on what you need to earn, and the hours you need to work to achieve your cake business success.

Don't forget this is not about working long hours and maybe losing your mind in the process just to make that last minute cake for a friend, or a cheap cake hunter.

No, you must have clearly defined working hours, rates of pay for yourself, profit margins and targets to achieve. Most of all you need to stick to them.

Do not be tempted to deviate from this the plan and sabotage your chances of reaching your cake business success, by taking on 'just a quick cake for a colleague or friend as money is money '. If you are continually chasing money, do you have a sustainable cake business and will there be anything left of you in a few years?

Whilst you are working on this last minute cake you are not marketing or networking with your ideal cake customers or working towards your clear goal.

If you were to deviate from your plan for cake business success, in terms of income goals, profit margins and hours of work, by accepting the colleagues or friends cake order, you could be like the cargo vessel in the above example.

If it deviated from its plotted course by just 1% the result, in the long run, would mean it ending up somewhere totally different from its intended destination, and so could you.

I am not saying don't accept the last minute cake in order terms of money, what I am saying is, that cake order will possibly be eating into your cake admin time or more importantly family time.

Therefore it is even more important that you define and understand your ideal cake customer. The Ideal cake customer that will pay you your worth so that you aren't tempted to top the bank account up and accept that last minute cake order.

Having a defined ideal cake customer also prevents you from slipping into the 'scattergun' approach to marketing.

If you use a 'scattergun' marketing strategy, you may not only be wasting your marketing budget, by reaching out to customers who are not interested in paying for a bespoke carefully crafted cake. You may be marketing to the ones who are quite happy to buy a supermarket cheaper mass produced cake, and it could also attract the cheap cake hunters too.

Defining who your ideal cake customers are helps you to employ target marketing in your cake business more effectively in terms of time and money.

It also assists you to locate that customer and reach out to them rather than by using the 'scattergun' marketing approach and hoping that you hit them with the spray.

(An example of scattergun marketing for me is placing an advert in a local newspaper, or a large leaflet drop on a housing estate.)

It is the first question I ask my cake business clients, my Cakepreneurs. I ask them who their ideal cake customers are, what do they look like in terms of gender, age, career, and where do they live etc. They need to be able to define them, and if not I assist them in doing so.

The more detail you get, the more you can understand your ideal cake customers to assist you in developing your cakes, cake products, your services and in fact your marketing to match their tastes and wants.

The more you can find out about your ideal customers the better. It is vital to understand them as this will help you with your cake business branding.

It is not by accident that we are talking about defining your ideal cake customers before we discuss branding for you and your cake business in chapter 4.

Let's Define Your Ideal Cake Customer

So hopefully you now understand that for your cake business to be a success, you need to define and find your ideal customer, so here's how I suggest you do it.

It is not fool proof and you will be amazed when a new ideal cake customer pops up from somewhere you have never thought of before. We continually learn and evolve in any business, not just the cake business, so don't forget to capture the information when this new ideal cake customer pops up. Where did they come from? What methods could you replicate to find another golden nugget of an ideal cake customer again

You may wish to read further on this subject, but I will give you a flavour of how to find your ideal cake customer.

I have heard ideal customer defining called, 'defining your avatars', or as I was taught, finding your 'Jane and or John Doe'. (Not very diverse at all, or inclusive, but I was taught business basics many moons ago.)

Now I prefer the term defining your ideal cake customer.

At this point whilst writing, I am chuckling to myself, because as I write this book in my office at my desk, my ideal customers are actually looking at me across the desk. I kid you not.

My ideal customers have names and faces. (Made up names and pictures cut out of magazines) but nevertheless, they are there with their information below their pictures, on A4 sheets, looking at me as I type. They are no doubt eyeing up the cherry coke and lemon drizzle cupcake on the desk!

I will burst the bubble a bit here, and add they are also known by a group letter too, which makes it quicker, and easier, on spreadsheets and mailing lists to define the customer groups they represent.

Why do I do this? Well, this ensures that when I am writing anything, this book, an email, a Facebook post etc., I can quickly scan my ideal customer profiles to ensure I am talking to everyone, or I can talk specifically to one ideal customer group.

For example, and chosen at random to highlight what I mean. You may have an ideal customer who like me may be in your 'Mr & Mr' or 'Mrs & Mrs' category.

I have one of these and it is called my 'Jason & Richard' category after my best friend Jason and his soon to be husband Richard.

I like trying to associate my ideal customer groups with actual people, as I feel that I am talking directly to them and I hope that this comes across in my communication style.

I will talk about branding in chapter 4, but your customer service, the way you talk to your cake customers, is what makes your cake business unique. It is your brand, so it is very important to take care and refine your communication style to suit your ideal cake customer group.

An example of this is I regularly receive an email from a supplier, which is addressed 'Dear Mr. Owner!'

I contacted the sender and asked that they changed their emails as I was a female and I found it quite offensive to be addressed as a male. The supplier apologised and said he couldn't do anything about is as it was the software they used to send out emails.

Needless to say, they have never had any custom from me!

I try, and fail, sometimes to be gender neutral in my language, as I think it makes me quite unique in the cake industry, as we do tend to be pink and fluffy and speak to ladies when let's face it some of the best cake decorators in the UK and the world are men, and I'm pretty sure men buy cakes too.

So let's talk about how we go about defining our ideal cake customer. I always start with a standard list of questions as a template.

- Age Range
- Highest Percentage of Gender in the group Male or Female
- Dietary Requirements
- Where do they live
- Where do they 'hang out '
- What brands do they like
- What is their preferred form of communication
- What does their day entail
- What are their challenges & frustrations/pain points
- What makes them happy

So let's explore what I mean by the above. Some of the categories are self-explanatory. Dietary requirements, this may be vegan, vegetarian, dairy or alcohol-free or eggless.

You may wish to remove this as a subcategory and make a separate ideal customer for each dietary requirement if you are going to explore these niche cake markets.

Or like me, you may wish to steer well clear as I did when asked for gluten-free cakes. (I felt it was too much of a responsibility if I got it wrong. Coeliac Disease is a horrid illness and one grain of gluten can cause major complications. I would pass that cake order over to a lady I knew who specialised in gluten-free.)

Where do they hang out means which social media channels, hairdressers/barbers, deli or nursery/ school, gym or health club etc?

The preferred form of communication means text, Facebook message, WhatsApp, or email. (Although I tried to be prescriptive on the communications channels I would reply to!)

Looking at their day, they may be a career type, on the 7am-7pm commute, work, commute cycle, or they may be a stay at home carers of children or parents.(The carer being the hardest job in the world may I add.)

Challenges and frustrations are good. Your ideal cake customer may want to be seen to be the best mom/dad in the world, balancing a career with parenthood. How can you and your cake business help them?

What is the extra service that you can provide that makes their life less stressful? Maybe you can offer them a children's cupcake decorating party as well as the cake. You could also sort the goody bags and hall decoration for them for the event.

Now I'm not suggesting for one second that you do all of this yourself, apart from the cupcake decorating party maybe.

(You will need to have costed this up as a package, and have the correct insurance, but it is an income stream worth costing up).

I'm trying to get you to think outside of the cake box here.

This concept my beautiful business partner Jo called 'and do you want to add fries with that!' I love that woman.

Perhaps make yourself a list of other complementary businesses that your cake business could work with. Children's party planners are a great compatible business.

You can pass on the work, or outsource the extra work yourself with commission. It has worked well for me in the past.

In relation to question 6, narrow this down to clothing and homeware stores. Where do they buy their clothes/ household accessories, or more importantly given the choice and the money where would they buy them from?

Now I'm a bargain hunter, but given the choice, and endless cash I am a Laura Ashley shopper. My home reflects Laura Ashley style. Silvers, metallic, pastel hints etc.

(If you decide to do a wedding consultation in the customer's home, it may give you a massive clue as to their tastes and what their colour pallet is if you look at their decor)

Challenges and frustrations - maybe they want to be able to bake easy home bakes like lemon drizzle cakes etc., in order to be seen as the perfect parent or partner.(You can maybe help them on your Facebook page to achieve this with hints and tips)

You can go one step further and create 'mood boards' for these ideal cake customer groups, with pictures and colours and designs of what they like.

In order to build these ideal customer profiles, you need information which you can start to gather straight away.

You may not have started your cake business yet or if you have taken some time to carry out this task which I feel again is vital to your cake business success.

It is not a one-stop exercise, it does need to be revisited and added to regularly. It depends on how successful you want your marketing and product development to be leading you to your successful cake business.

It is no use thinking you want to develop a line in black and white cakes, for example, because you like a cake that you saw. Your cake designs should be what the ideal customer group wants, in terms of style and colour palate as well as cake flavourings. So it is best to try and find out what that is for your individual ideal cake customer group.

Now you are probably thinking this seems like too much hard work already and you will just go with the flow of what everybody else is doing i.e. naked or drip cakes.

This is all well and good, but it is not going to make you unique and stand out from the crowd.

By all means, provide the naked and or drip cakes, but make the style your own Use what you have learned in terms of colour and style from your ideal cake customer groups.

Even if you only do a fraction of what I have described above you will reap the benefits. Do it all and you really are taking your cake business seriously and focusing on your goal of cake business success.

If you want to be a success in the cake business you should be focusing on your goal and vision every day and asking yourself 'What have I done today to work towards that success'.

Even if it was five minutes planning your social media marketing, checking on your books and income targets, learning a new technique on the internet, anything that is on your roadmap to make you a success, but achieve at least one thing a day

You could use a free online app called Survey Monkey to develop a questionnaire to post on Facebook or mail to your mailing list

Ask the questions outlined above, in a more articulate way perhaps, but ensure you put a price bracket section for the maximum price they are willing to pay for ' a bespoke piece of original sugar craft art crafted by a cake professional' ...You!

Give them a choice of two price brackets, but ensure you include your average maximum cake price. Then when the replies come back discount those that replied with the lower cake bracket replies, as these are not your ideal customers.

I was shown a trick the other day regarding pricing in a restaurant. Put an absolutely ridiculous price bracket as the first choice and then the lower prices below that. You will find that the average price your ideal cake customer will pay may increase if there is a very high priced cake bracket displayed.

You could give away a box of luxury cupcakes, at the least, for this valuable information, from your cake business, by holding a draw of all those who have responded to your survey.

A word of warning though, response rates to surveys are always extremely low, between 10-20%, so make sure you ask as many as potential ideal cake customers as possible to take part, in order to get a meaningful reply.

Don't forget to use the gifting of the winner's box of cupcakes to your best advantage, and get a photograph and them tagged on all your social media etc. (There is more online marketing advice in chapter 7)

I would suggest carrying out this online survey at least a couple of times a year as your email list grows.

Maybe if you are brave enough, stand outside a store in your ideal chosen cake selling areas, such as Marks & Spencer's, Waitrose, or House of Fraser, and carry out a clipboard survey too.

Vary the times and days, but ensure that you give them your leaflet and you look the part.

(You may need permission to do this from the shopping mall owners or local council. But it doesn't stop school kids with their teachers doing it quite regularly down my high street and I'm sure they haven't got permission!)

Don't forget there is more than one type of ideal customer so if you are doing the clipboard thing ask different people from different age ranges and gender etc.

What Does Your Ideal Cake Customer Want From You

What else can we find out about our ideal cake customers?

So hopefully you have carried out a survey to find out a bit more about your ideal cake customers, the ones who will pay you your worth for your cakes.

There is no harm actually picking up the phone and talking to an existing ideal customer, and having a good old natter to ascertain a bit more information.

Give them a call when you think it may be convenient, and ask for feedback on their cake and perhaps ask them what more you could offer them more in the future. Value their feedback and thoughts.

Tell them you are trying to develop more cake products, and ask them to answer some quick questions, or if you can, send them the survey. I always find that an open ended chat framed by the questionnaire works well.

Once you have a good selection of responses to your survey to find your ideal cake customers try and see what brands they actually like. If you have a number of clothing brands in your responses I would suggest you go and have a look at those clothing stores and take a look at their social media and websites.

The colours and textures used, the style, maybe simple and elegant, natural and earthy, or vintage, to name but a few. But this will be evident from looking in these places and may assist you in developing your next cake design.

This information may show you how that particular brand is addressing its customer's frustrations, their 'pain points', and they may be using certain language to speak to their customers.

Let's face it, these big brands have invested a vast amount of money in learning to speak to their customers, and you in your cake business can be very grateful for all the hard work they have done in assisting you. with your cake business.

So now we can develop our ideal customer mood boards a bit further by pinning colours and textures to it. Stepping back a bit we could actually extend our clipboard questionnaire to showing our potential ideal customers colour palettes like the free colour paint brochures found in hardware stores. We can build an even more in-depth picture of our ideal client likes and dislikes by seeing their colour choices. This is brilliant yet again for developing our new cakes.

Don't forget if the majority of customers pick pastels and one or two choose a black and white palette you know you can discount the black and white as a choice for your next cake collection as the sample size will be too low.

Once again one of my Cakepreneur clients discovered a new ideal client in the eggless Sikh wedding cake market which wasn't being catered for in her local area, although there was a thriving and expanding Sikh community in it, which had to travel quite a way to find cake suppliers who made eggless cakes.

I will congratulate this client once again as she immersed herself in finding out as much as she could about this ideal customer group by using the bride who had actually approached her.

She was able to use the questionnaire to build a healthy and full cake customer profile with colours, designs, and flavours etc. by actually spending time with her customer. It just goes to show we can't always use technology, social media, to find out what you need to know about your ideal customers. You actually have to go out there sometimes and walk in their shoes.

I mentioned my one of my best friends Jason who is getting married in August 2018 to his fiancé, Richard.

I managed to catch up with Jason last week regarding their forthcoming nuptials and asked how they went about finding their wedding cake maker/supplier. I think it is important to capture this as an interview with an ideal cake customer, and therefore I have outlined our conversation below.

I must add that the wedding is very high end. It must be as the invite gives me a telephone number to pre-arrange parking my helicopter!

Here's how it went:

CBC: "Congratulations Jason once again, and I bet you and Richard are so well organised and ready for your big day. Can you tell me how you went about choosing your wedding cake maker?"

Jason: "Well we spent months looking through Pinterest, deciding what we didn't want and eventually decided on a macaron tower. We didn't want to go down the traditional wedding cake route, and have lots of cake left over afterwards. We were looking for something very sophisticated but nothing too masculine or feminine in design.

We searched on Google and found a few suppliers for our tower, and began the process of locating our supplier.

We wanted to choose a cake business with strong community values and ethics, as this is important to us. Our actual chosen wedding tower supplier is a champion for a few causes, and she actively supports a number of worthwhile charities.

Her customer service was second to none. We were actually going with another supplier, but their customer service was appalling. It seemed as though we were an inconvenience when it came to choosing colours and flavours. This other supplier took ages to answer our calls or return our emails, and when we went to collect our pre-arranged macaron samples, the staff in her shop knew nothing about them, and didn't seem bothered. This occurred on two occasions so it wasn't a genuine mistake!

So we began our search for a new supplier. We found one hundreds of miles away in Edinburgh and we chatted on the telephone and instantly we clicked and felt reassured. Nothing seemed too much trouble for her, she has made us feel very special. We felt confident that she will make it happen on the day and we do not have to worry. Her flavours and macarons are the best I have ever tasted!

As you can see from Richard and Jason's experience, values, ethics, and communication were key to finding their wedding cake supplier.

Customer service is also key.

This one simple interview gives me a lot of information about one of my ideal cake customer groups, and I hope you can pick up on what is important to them.

A simple phone call gave me all this information.

Hopefully, I will post pictures of the macaron tower, and the actual wedding on my Facebook page 'The Cake Biz Coach' at the end of the summer, as I join Jason and Richard in celebrating this very special day.

(Note: If you are wondering why I didn't make Jason and Richards wedding cake/macaron tower. Well I have been invited to 5 very special weddings this year and I want to enjoy the preparation and the actual weddings themselves. I never mix business with pleasure and I am resisting being asked to make my daughter's wedding cake as we speak.)

So you know who your ideal cake customers are, as you have hopefully carried out the 'defining your ideal cake customers' work from earlier.

You will now have done the work to identify what they like and want in terms of colours, textures, and styles. This will help you to communicate with them by helping you to develop your brand, your website, and your social media.

It will also assist you to build a rapport and more importantly develop your cakes along the lines, that will attract your ideal customers.

Maybe a little reminder here of why we are seeking the ideal cake customer. They are the ones who will pay you your worth, won't haggle on the price, and will be a delight to work with!

Next, you need to know how you can effectively communicate with your ideal cake customers, to show them that you are unique, you care, so that they can gain trust and confidence in you to deliver their perfect cake!

Now I know this is only chapter 3, and you are heading for the kettle thinking I just want to make cakes and sell them, what is all this heavy business stuff it's not me!

Don't worry I felt exactly the same, and so did a few of my cake business coaching clients, when they first started.

I want to give you insider knowledge that will take you to success with your cake business. Even if you only make a few tweaks to your existing cake business, I'm sure after reading this book, you will see a measurable difference.

If you haven't even started your cake business yet and you are still in the planning stage this business knowledge will give you a real head start to hit the road to success quickly.

Remember Chapter 1, "WE ARE BUSINESS OWNERS WHOSE PRODUCT IS CAKE!"

So grab that cuppa if you need it, and let's settle back and find out about how to effectively communicate with our ideal cake customers.

Effectively communication is not about the hard sell, as I am sure you are like me and not a fan of the hard sell or sales scripts.

What I actually mean is how to effectively communicate with your ideal cake customer to build you a unique relationship with them.

'People buy People' and this is so true for the cake business.

How to Talk Your Ideal Cake Customers Language

When you are standing at a wedding fair, amongst three other wedding cakes suppliers, you need a unique selling point for your cake business, or an edge to get your ideal cake customer interested and ordering from you.

Have you ever been into a store or talked to someone on the telephone, with you as the potential customer, and gone away thinking the condescending ****.

(Makes me chuckle, as I always think of the film 'Pretty Woman' when this happens, the bit where she walks into the clothing store, and they look down their nose at her.)

Well, maybe that is an extreme case.

You need to build up a rapport with your potential ideal cake customer right from the start, and by using the correct language you can help this along.

Back to my science bit again.

We all have an unconscious preference hidden in our rains for communicating in a specific way believe it or not.

Your unconscious mind has a communication style with which it communicates to your potential cake customers.

It may not be an intentional communication style but it means the language we use is very important.

In the Neuro-Linguistic Programming (NLP), models of communication * (bear with me, it is how we take in, filter, process and understand information from the outside world inside our own heads.

It hugely affects our thoughts and behaviors. Quite a heavy subject for us cakey people, but in business and sales terms it is massive.

Understanding communication styles, help big businesses relate to their customers and build a rapport with them. It is well worth taking a look at NLP if you want to take your communication and rapport building skills in business, to the next level.

Basically, there are different groups of people. Visual, Auditory, Kinesthetic (feeling) and Auditory Digital (very logical people).There is also Olfactory (smell), and Gustatory (taste).

The latter two are useful at a wedding fair or wedding cake consultation where the smell of freshly baked warm cake, and or having a taste of your delicious cakes, may speak volumes to potential cake customers

As a successful cake business owner, it is important that we talk to every one of the above filters in a potential cake customers sub consciousness, and be mindful of the language we use.

By language I mean the words and language we use in our emails, social media channels, and our websites, even when talking to potential cake customers on the telephone.

We are all taught to treat people like we want to be treated!

Well, I'm going to say forget that, when trying to communicate with your ideal cake customers.

Actually, treat people in the way they want to be treated. Making sure you talk (write) to customers in their preferred communication style. This makes it easier to build a rapport by communicating with the customer's subconscious.

If you look deeper into this amazing art, and the science of communicating, you will see that you and your customers may have quite a few characteristics/filters in their heads filtering our communications with them at the same time!

Right, that's the science behind building a rapport with communication styles. Here are a few examples to outline what I mean.

With a 'Visual' person a statement like - "I can see what you are saying about the cake", or "can you see what I mean about the cake?"

With an 'Auditory' person a statement like - "I can hear what you are saying about the cake", or "I can hear your excitement about the design of your wedding cake."

Kinesthetic person - "I can feel that you are happy with that design", or "how do you feel about my cake design?"

Auditory Digital Person - "Your specifications are clear and I am confident I can meet your requirements", or, "I think you will find my cakes are a great value and high quality."

This is a very simple overview of how using specific words in sentences reaches into the sub consciousness of a potential customer.

The simplest way to approach all of the above is to ensure your text encompasses all the four main groups' ones above.

Here is an example:

Phrases like - "Thank you for your cake enquiry. I can see that you are excited about the designs on my website, and I feel that perhaps our Two-Tier Unicorn Cake would suit your occasion very well. I look forward to hearing from you regarding the attached quote."

This paragraph covers the main three groups and will hopefully give you a few pointers on building a rapport with your ideal client.

As I have said in the first three chapters, the cake business is a business, and I do not apologise for my 'go hard or go home' attitude to it.

I want nothing more than for you to succeed in the cake business, using the techniques and tricks that the big boys and girls use in their businesses every day but get charged thousands for the pleasure.

In later chapters, you will learn more about heart to heart 'H2H' marketing, where we are again trying to build up that rapport with our ideal cake customers.

For now, though, I think it time to talk about branding where you can use all you have discovered so far to assist building an effective brand for your successful cake business.

'THE SECRET TO SUCCESS IS YOUR MINDSET - Justin Bryant'

'THE SECRET TO CAKE BUSINESS SUCCESS IS WITHIN YOURS AND YOUR IDEAL CAKE CUSTOMERS MIND' - Diana Catherine. The Cake Biz Coach.

For me to be the best cake business coach I can, I will continue to learn and use all the resources available to me to make sure I can support and guide you to running a successful cake business.

I have studied NLP briefly and see its worth in business, especially with customer rapport building. My attempts above do not even scratch the surface of what NLP can do.

I am not an expert in NLP, and I rely on experts like Marcus Filler from Confidence Works, who is highly qualified and he guides and supports me.

Thank you to Marcus for your assistance in my ongoing learning on this fascinating subject. Marcus can be found at www.confidence-works.co.uk

Developed by Tad James & Wyatt Woodsmall (1988) from work by Richard Bandler & John Grinder (1975

Chapter 4. Stand Out From the Crowd

Why is Branding Your Cake Business Important

If you have already started a cake business or you are thinking about it, again I cannot stress how important branding is. Branding is key!

Branding can be compared to the good solid foundations of a house before any brick is laid on the main house.

Lots of cake business owners skip over this first essential step to building a successful cake business and end up being unfairly bundled in with the cheap cake makers.

You need to stand out from the crowd on day one.

Without considering branding you risk launching your cake business into, or running your business with the herd!

As I mentioned before you and your cake business as a minimum, should be instantly identifiable by your colour brand, which should run through your website (if you have one) social media, leaflets, even photographs of you.

If you are already running a cake business, ask yourself if it is delivering your dream and vision? Are you happy that you are on course to deliver on your goals?

If not maybe it is time to step back, and maybe look at a rebrand!

Don't be worried by a rebrand. When you stop and think about it we have accepted many rebrands, from well-known household names over the years.

In relation to logo rebrands, did you even notice Instagram rebranded in 2016, after its launch in 2010. The old logo was a camera, and now it has a new white camera outline, on a vivid rainbow of orange, pink, purples and yellow.

Morrison's, the supermarket, has also started its rebrand by rolling out their new logo. They have added 'since 1899' underneath their name, and a yellow tree, or is it an ear of wheat, above it.

In 2018 The Co-Op has also rebranded its logo, going back to the design they first had many moons ago, which was called 'the cloverleaf' by some.

There are many more I could list such as Guinness, Coke, McDonalds, but it is an accepted practice that businesses evolve, their brands evolve, so it may be time to see if your cake business brand and logo is up to date, and says all it can about you and your cake business.

If you haven't started your cake business yet, don't hang around trying to develop the best logo you can. My advice is go with good, as it can evolve, and it can be altered as you get more into your cake business.

Next, there is your brand in terms of your cake businesses name.

We have also accepted many changes in brand names over the years. If you are as old as I am you may remember Marathon chocolate bars, which became Snickers overnight.

Cushelle toilet tissue, which was formerly Charmin, and the Dime Bar was rebranded as a Daim Bar, and Immac became Veet in 2003.

See how easily we accept name changes in business.

All rather interesting, but the point I am trying to make is that if your cake business is not attracting your ideal cake customers, who appreciate your cakes, and will pay you your worth, then it is maybe time to rebrand.

You can rebrand your cake business by carrying out the research I outlined in chapter 3. Map out the details of your ideal cake customer. Consider a new logo and even a name. A fresh start for your cake business.

Don't worry about your existing cake customers not being able to find you after your rebrand, as I'm sure your phone number won't change and you can inform everyone via email/text or via your social media of the change, just like all the big brands do.

Branding as I have said previously is not just in your business name or your logo, it is everything. It's you, your cakes, your customer service, the way you treat customers, everything.

It's everything that sets you apart from any other high-end professional cake business in your chosen selling area.

You could be concentrating on a niche cake market, like eggless wedding or naked cakes, it matters not, you may need to look at your brand in order to make your cake business a success.

I am actually a big fan of developing your cake business in a niche market as the old saying goes 'Jack of all trades master of none'.

It may be something that develops as your cake business evolves and you find a niche, or it finds you. Never say never in the cake business.

Here's a thought.

Mixing celebration cakes and high-end wedding cakes under one business name may be detrimental to your brand!

You could consider having two or more brands for your cake business. Think of them as mini- cake businesses. This could help bring clarity to your marketing, enabling you to target your marketing more effectively.

Again this is not a rule, but a consideration.

If it is cake business success you want then maybe step back and take a look at your cake business, if you are already running one, or ask someone else you trust to take a look.

It could be that having your cakes under all one brand is addressing all the needs and wants of your ideal cake customers, but never dismiss splitting your cake business into more than one brand. Celebration cakes in one and high-end wedding cakes in another.

You need to create, what the big design company's call, a 'Destination 'brand. A cake business that your ideal cake customers wants and needs to buy from and other similar businesses want to collaborate with, such as wedding florists, photographers etc.

It's not going to happen overnight, but with your mind set firmly focused on your goal of making your cake business a success, you should be ready to look at branding your cake business.

You want your cake business brand to be identifiable anywhere by its colours and style.

Now just because your statement cakes on your website, and social media, are reflective of your cake brand doesn't mean that you will not be taking a commission for any other type of cake outside of your brand identity. Your statement cakes are to show your styling and your professional work.

Again if your branding isn't delivering you your ideal cake customer willing to pay you your worth for your cakes, which in turn will help you to achieve your goals, then take a step back and consider a rebrand.

Don't worry, you can carry on working with, and in, the old brand until your new cake brand is ready to launch. (I will talk about launching or launching your cake business in chapter 6).

The right branding for your cake business cannot help but attract the right ideal cake customer.

I took a course on branding again many years ago, and the coach asked the class to take a step back and ask ourselves what we were selling in our individual businesses.

Cake I thought!

Well yes, but no.

Yes cakes, but the coach asked us to put our products, cakes for me, in the centre of a piece of paper and to draw labels around it, in a clock face pattern, stating what we wanted our customers to feel and experience when they purchased our products. My cakes.

She then said If we had difficulty thinking of these labels, then we were to think of the feeling you would get if we woke one morning and there was a top of the range brand new car sitting on the drive, with all the bells and whistles, and a big silk bow with our name on a label hanging off it.

Do you get the feeling? Maybe its joy you would feel, as you know you have been given a quality product, with the best workman/woman ship.

Maybe excitement and contentment! I know I would feel very special.

This is the feeling, she said, she wanted my customers to feel when they picked up or I delivered their cakes.

It was then that I understood that it is branding and marketing that will assist them to feel this way.

Imagine walking into Selfridges and selecting a set of white cotton bedding. You know the price will be premium, but I bet you have made purchases at this high-end store or others like it such as Lewis's, before.

In your mind, you have the knowledge that you could purchase very good serviceable white cotton bedding, on the internet, at perhaps a cheaper price, but it gives you that warm glow when you walk out with that Selfridges bag... a little bit of luxury, you feel, because you deserve it.

You maybe know the quality that John Lewis stands from their branding and marketing.

Well, brand yourself carefully so that you can hopefully give your cake customers that same warm glow.

Your website, Facebook, and other social media sites are your shop window, your selling environment which you can use to showcase your brand.

Ask yourself, would you expect customers to pay top prices for cakes being sold from a paste table at a car boot sale, or from a cake advert on Gumtree?

Next imagine you have been given the free rental of a store for your cake business on a top high street, with an open cheque book to brand and decorate it. (Who has cheque books these days, but you know what I mean)

I'm sure you may get a top designer to do the branding work and your cake shop will look very high end.

I can't help thinking of Peggy Porschen Cakes Ltd. here, and her fabulous bakery in Belgravia, London. A very strong high-end brand.

But unfortunately you may not have a shop, or the store and an open cheque book, and therefore your web presence is your cake shop, and the good news is it won't cost you a fortune to look 'the business' and attract the right cake customers... Branding is the key.

How to go about Creating Your Brand or Rebrand

So you are now taking branding seriously and you are going to work out what your cake brand looks, feels and sounds like.

I have mentioned being a 'Jack of all trades, master of none'

Branding is now part and parcel of my business advice to my cake business students, my Cakepreneurs.

I'm am not an expert in branding though. I know enough and do my research, but I do have an excellent interior designer on my Cake Biz Coach team of experts, who I bounce ideas off, as she's the one with the degree in this subject. She also happens to love cake.

So bit of transparency there to show you I take the best advice, and surround myself with experts so that I can help you with your cake business.

To begin with, it might help you if you decide which of these words defines what you want your ideal customer to think of your cake business.

Don't forget we are aiming for a professional persona here. This list is just an example, you could come up with your own word.

Try and find a word, or more words, that define what you want your brand to feel like.

An example would be elegant, classic, vintage, romantic, futuristic, unusual, floral, monotone, natural

Don't forget we are aiming for a professional persona here. This list is just an example, you could come up with your own words.

You may want to show a sample of family and friends a selection of pictures of other web pages, not necessarily cake businesses, that look and feel how you want your cake business to feel.

(For me that would be Laura Ashley or John Lewis magazine pictures and products.)

Ask the audience, your family and friends, to describe how they feel about those other businesses from the websites or pictures, and ask them why they make them feel that way. This may help you define a word or words for your cake business brand.

When I look at John Lewis I think crisp, clean contemporary and elegant as an example. You may see something different.

Next, after the words you have chosen to describe your cake brand, is the colours.

This is also an area of branding that is so important, you may need to go and research it, as it will fill a book, quite literally.

The science behind the power of colour psychology in branding, and indeed marketing, is huge. Many colour psychologists talk about colours in branding being divided into seasons!

This doesn't mean the brand colours reflects the season you are in, it means that your cake brand suggests a particular season.

Colour brand psychologists talk about 'the spring personality' which has characteristics of bright, energetic, bubbly on trend, colours.

There are some less desirable qualities too in the spring brand personality, but the colours of a spring personality, taken from spring flowers and the pastel shades of late spring blossoms reflect the colours of spring.

Or there is the summer personality etc. These colour seasons are well worth reading up on.

It is best to decide which season, as far as colour psychology, defines you and what you want your cake customers to see and feel about your cake business.

The colour seasons continue with autumn and winter colour personalities too.

Hard to imagine a winter colour personality being the brand colours for a cake business, but it is possible as they can say expensive and lavish.

Winter personality colours are strong and bold from deep red of winter berries to other bold shades, and it is the only one that includes black in its palette.

Right, this is all a bit too deep, but I have hopefully given you a flavour or appetite to learn more about colour psychology in the cake business.

But I will make it easier for you.

If you go to a paint store, or a DIY store and pick up a paint colour chart, you will begin to see the colour palettes grouped into these seasonal personality colours, it really is quite fascinating.

These charts are really useful because if you are like me, and rubbish at identifying complementary colours, they come in handy when developing new designs for cakes and with establishing your brand colour identity.

Maybe it is time to take a look at the top 50 top cake businesses again, and see if you can define their personality by their colour choices.

Now this is expert stuff but I'm sure you will find some great examples, but with others, you will find them wanting, maybe.

It's now time for a bit of cutting and sticking, or if you are a millennial, copy and pasting. It's mood board time, cakey people.

In order to create your brand identity and your cake collection, you will need to nail your colour personality. If the research you did above still hasn't sunk in or born fruit, then try complementing it with a mood board.

Find magazines and photographs of an object in your desired colour personality palate. The objects and things don't have to be cake related.

(I sometimes see things on the television that inspire me, and I end up taking screenshots of the TV...)

Now it's a fine balance here of what you want, and what your ideal customer wants from a cake business brand in terms of colour identity.

Pinterest is great for collecting colours and ideas for your branding. Again I have mood boards on my Pinterest with everything from kettles to blankets in my brand colours.

If you have done the work with your ideal cake customer from chapter 3, you will have an idea of what colour palates your ideal cake customer gravitates to.

Your ideal cake customers may have mentioned brands they like and you can see the colour palette of those brands from their websites.

Hopefully, this is aligned with what you want to represent your brand colours.

If not, you have a choice to make, either to align with your ideal cake customers colours or go with yours, and be unique.

Don't be surprised if your cake order book isn't as full as you wan,t as you have gone against your ideal customers colour comfort area, but hopefully you might have dangled some bait and a new ideal cake customer will be tempted by your cake brand colours.

You can always revisit this colour branding if you need to. Again just to reiterate on colour branding.

Your colour branding for your website and social media etc, will also be reflected in your statement cake collections hopefully, or in the staging and backdrops used to photograph your cakes.

That is not to say if an ideal customer comes along and wants a purple and black spotted four tier wedding cake that you refuse to make it.

If they are willing to pay you your worth then, of course, deliver their heart's desire, although you may think twice about putting it on your social media. Or maybe you do put it on your social media and it opens up a whole new ideal cake customer niche for you.

These 'different' colours may not be to your taste but there is obviously a market for them maybe, as long as they are your ideal customers and pay you your worth.

Naming Your Cake Business and Logos

I'm always being asked questions in relating to setting up a cake business, but the question I get asked most often is " what shall I call myself? "

Now I have to ask myself, who am I to advise you here, as I have previously made the mistake of not thinking a cake business name through. In fact, when Jo and I set up The Cake Decorating Academy seven years ago we called ourselves Buttercream and Bows!

Now that didn't say cake decorating school did it!

(Mind you we weren't alone as apparently 'Apple' sells phones and laptops etc., and 'Sky' is a TV Channel and 'Virgin' and airline!)

But having realised our error and lived with it, I can now pass on the little nuggets of advice I have gathered and learned along the way, in relation to naming your cake business.

But I strongly recommend that you make it clear you are a cake making business.

Something too general such as 'Diana's Creations' may make it difficult for people searching online for a cake maker in their area.

Whereas 'Diana's Cake Creations' gives an indication of what your business might have to offer.

This doesn't have to be quite as straightforward as having the word cake in your business name, but including a reference to cakes, cake decorating, baked goods or pastries will certainly be helpful to cake customers trying to find you.

The next thing you need to consider when choosing your cake business name, is giving yourself room to grow, as you don't want to limit yourself in the future.

'My Cake Pop Company' might sound tempting, but what happens in five years' time when you want to add cupcakes and wedding cakes to your cake portfolio.

My cake pops, cupcakes and wedding cakes doesn't have the same ring to it, and is far too long. You may already be offering cupcakes and wedding cakes, but your name doesn't suggest this.

Therefore don't limit the future success of your cake business by using a name that is too specific or shuts the door to expanding your cake portfolio in the future.

Legally there is only a limitation on limited company (Ltd.) names in the UK, and those business names protected by copyright, and trademark.

Best to check with Companies House to make sure your chosen name is not already registered as a business and check for any copyright name infringement.

If you are a sole trader there is no limitation on what you call your cake business, as far as Companies House is concerned, as you don't have to register with them. There may be the copyright infringement though!

There can, of course, be a 'Pandora's Little Cake Creations' in every town and village of the UK, if you are a sole trader.

This gets a wee bit confusing though when potential cake customers are trying to search for your cake business on the internet.

They may come across a 'Pandora's Little Cake Creations' in another town which might not have the same branding, ethics or values as your cake business. It may have a poor website and its reviews may not be great either. So be aware. It's the risk you take.

Plus it is possible that the domain name on the internet is already taken together with the social media names for the Pandora's Little Cake Creations.

Once again it is essential that you check for any trademark and copyrighted names too as you want to ensure you are original and safe legally.

Family names are safe, if sometimes boring.

Carters Bakery, Jones Cake Shop etc. Maybe not the most creative method of a naming a cake business, but it does get the job done.

Try and avoid quirky business names as they can be polarising.

Some start off by being cute but get very stale quickly. As a general rule of thumb, avoid names that will be embarrassing every time you answer the phone.

(I'm not going to give examples here as I don't want to offend anyone but I think you get what I mean!)

There are a few naming formulas that have worked for others cake businesses, in the past, so if all else fails, give them a try.

Object + Product = Red Door Cakes, Bluebird Cakes, Passion Flower Cakes; Or

Geographical + Product = Four Oaks Celebration Cakes, North Lane Cakes, Little Venice Cake Company*

I would suggest going back to the branding exercise and see what colours you are going to use for your branding and perhaps choose an object from that colour palette.

Bluebell Cakes, Sunflower Cakes, The Pastel Pink Cake Company, White Lily Cakes, Silk Orchid Cake Company. I hope you are getting the idea.

But whatever you do don't limit your brand straight away. If you are not 100 % sure that you will only be supplying one cake product such as macarons, cupcakes or cake pops in the future, then once again don't limit yourself.

Maybe use your own name.

Diana Catherine - Bespoke Wedding Cake Artist

Diana Catherine - Sugar craft Artist and Wedding Cake Specialist

Once you have settled on a name it's now time to look for or design a logo.

Logos are easily identifiable symbols, text and or images that represent your cake business as a unique brand.

Logos are very important as they say 'Emily's Couture Cake Company 'in one small symbol or group of words.

Having a logo for your cake business is non-negotiable really in my mind.

Take a look at those websites and brands that you identified with when you were choosing your brand colours. What does their logo say about them?

Remember we spoke about the Morrison's rebrand, and how they had incorporated 'since 1899' in their logo.

Maybe this was to give a sense of how well established they are. The ear of wheat, or is it a golden tree (I'm not sure), which they have now included in their new logo, does it make you think of natural products from the earth perhaps.

* Little Venice Cake Company belongs to Mitch Turner.

You can design your logo yourself or get a friend to do, it or maybe outsource your logo designing. Remember though that it is your brand, your cake business success bus and you are driving it, so be prescriptive if you outsource this.

There are numerous people and companies, on the internet, who will design your cake business logo and charge around £25 or less.

But don't hang about though with making or with the design of your logo, and wait until it's perfect, just pick one and go with it. Too many cake businesses never progress as the owners get bogged down in 'false busy' tasks.

Logos are very important as they say 'Emily's Couture Cake Company' in one small symbol or group of words.

So enjoy creating your logo or branding your cake business with a new logo but don't take too long. Go with good and move on as you can get lost in rebranding and take your eye off cake business success.

Creating Your Cake Collections and Business Plans

Now apart from "What shall I name my cake business?" and "How do I price my cakes?" the next two questions are amongst the ones I get asked quite regularly by my cake business students.

"Do I need a business plan to start my cake business?"

Well, most people think a business plan is to enable you to get a business loan to start your cake business.

I would suggest that you don't need a bank loan to start or grow a cake business, as it is relatively cheap to start up one up, and the success methods in this book are relatively cheap too.

Plus if you have been, or are, a hobby caker, I would suggest that you have most of what you need, in terms of equipment, already.

But I strongly believe that it is good practice to draw up a business plan, for your cake business whether you are starting out or have been running it for a while.

I am forever grateful to Jo Gilbert, a fantastic business strategist, who made me see the value of a great business plan, helping me to achieve my goals. Whether it is a small cake business or a multinational company it matters not a business plan will focus you on achieving your cake business success.

Jo Gilbert has taught me that every business needs a business plan '...... to show you that your business is viable and sustainable for years to come ...'

She also taught me that a business plan is a living document, and that it evolves, and changes and it should be reviewed weekly or monthly to ensure you are on track to meet your goals and vision of success in your cake business.

Jo Gilbert can be found at www.jogilbert.co.uk

One of the most important parts of any business plan, I feel, is the mission statement. Now don't be afraid, it's not complicated.

I believe your cake business mission statement sits shoulder to shoulder, so to speak, with your goal and vision in terms of its importance in your planning.

Your mission statement is a short summary of the aims and values of your cake business so that you, your ideal cake customer and anyone you employ or outsource tasks to, such as social media, can clearly see them.

If you do employ anyone, whether it is for a few hours a week, or you outsource, then make sure that they buy into your mission statement. Put it up clearly where you can see it daily and definitely display it in your shop window, social media and or website.

Keep it clear and concise. Look at the values that your ideal cake customers may have. For example do they want you to be philanthropic and supportive of local causes etc.? Remember that this was important to Richard and Jason I mentioned earlier, when they were choosing their wedding cake supplier.

Here is one example:

"To passionately design and create unique professionally handcrafted wedding cakes to bring happiness and joy to the hearts and minds of our customers in their look, smell and taste - whilst focusing on a great customer service at all times"

Some more examples

"To inspire and nurture the human spirit- one person, one cup and one neighborhood at a time" Starbucks.

"To attract and attain customers with high valued products and services and the most satisfying ownership experience in America" Toyota Motor Sales U.S.A.

I do like the Toyota mission statement, but I am unsure as to whether I would make this a public one, as I feel uncomfortable with the 'high valued products' wording, but you can see it is short and sharp and to the point.

I suggest you invest some time on looking at business cases and at the very least produce your cake business mission statement.

The other question I am asked is

"How many cakes should I have in my portfolio?"

Well, the best answer is if you are starting out, enough to show your cake skills and abilities.

If you are just starting your cake business, just three showstopper cakes could be enough until you have built up your portfolio.

For those already running a business I think that ten cakes in your portfolio, is actually sufficient, or thereabouts, especially if its wedding cakes.

Now, fashions and colour palettes for cakes, come and go year after year, but I think as a general rule, at least half of your cakes in this portfolio, especially if they are wedding cakes, should be muted or neutral colours. Ivories, light pastel shades.

The rule is similar to selling a house. Every estate agent will tell you to decorate your home in neutral colours so that the buyers are not put off by your chosen colour scheme.

It does really all depend on your ideal cake customers though and what your research has told you about them. What colours and styles attract them?

But this does not mean you can't be original, and niche with your colours. No use being called 'The Rock and Roll Bride Cake Company' and using neutrals and pastel shades! Just be aware that you are narrowing your cake customer numbers by being niche in your colour schemes.

You may have already been running your cake business for a while, and the thought of bringing your portfolio down to ten cakes maybe a big ask. All I ask you to do is ask yourself the following questions before you dismiss a total or partial cake overhaul.

- Am I being paid my worth for my cakes, my skill and my time?
- Am I attracting the right cake customers who won't haggle over the price?
- Am I sick of working long hours and getting stressed?

Now reconsider an overhaul of your cake portfolio again.

It could be that your cake portfolio is amazing and you just need to tweak a few cakes or replace one to keep in with your outward facing branding.

Plan a year ahead in the cake business and try and design and bring out a new showstopper cake every six months if you can.

Maybe consider dropping an unpopular cake that isn't selling from your shop window (website, social media) during your six monthly reviews.

(It is essential that you build cake development time into your cake business. You maybe aren't going to be busy all the time, but hopefully, you are, and this is when you can develop your next showstopper cake for your portfolio).

Don't forget with your cake portfolio you are aiming for brand identity with your cakes. Your aim should be that anyone viewing a picture of your cakes should know that it is one of yours.

If you have sketched out your cake portfolio and identified techniques you have no experience of or you are a bit rusty with then maybe research the technique online or via a class or magazine. I personally love all the magazines that are out there at the moment especially Cake

Masters. Take a look if you haven't seen it. I love that you can order back copies of it with a technique you need.

A word of warning though. Some cake decorating techniques are more time consuming and more expensive in the ingredient costs. I.e. straight edge cakes with a chocolate ganache underneath for example.

It is worth considering when building a new cake portfolio is how well you are going to master a new technique, and will this new technique be far too time-consuming to begin with.

Maybe find another route to achieving the straight edge which is quicker and not as expensive, or maybe steer clear of a technique altogether!

Now I'm not saying scrimp on the cost of ingredients here, when trying to find another technique to produce a particular look, as this is never a good idea. I am just suggesting caution when developing your cake portfolio to consider your skill gaps, your ability, and time to learn and become competent in a new cake techniques.

There is of course outsourcing part of your new cake design if needed.

For example, I am not the quickest in the world at sugar craft flowers particularly large ones that need colouring. My ME causes difficulty with my hands, these days, and I don't get as much practice as I used to, and this slows me down.

If I were to develop a cake for my cake portfolio, with a signature sugar craft flower on, then I might consider outsourcing the sugar craft flower part to an expert who lives locally, as she loves making them, she is an award winner, and is much quicker and therefore it would be better for my cake business to commission her to make a complex sugar craft flower these days.

Chapter 5: Pricing Your Cakes

Pricing Structures

There is no other emotive subject in the cake business world than pricing your cakes.

There are quite a few methods and strategies for pricing your cakes, and as an active member of many Facebook cake groups, for a number of years, I am amazed that the same question is still being asked over and over again, all these years later.

You know the one. You see a post with a picture of a beautiful cake and the question "How Much Should I Charge?"

This is usually attached to a very sorry story about a difficult customer who has challenged the cake maker's price on the cake, and is battering them on text over the cost of the cake!

Well, this stops here!

When deciding on a pricing structure for your cake business, you must understand that you have designed and lovingly created a bespoke cake, to your customer's specifications, and that your price point will reflect all your hard work, your skill, your expertise, and passion. The price is an essential part of how your cake business will be perceived.

Therefore in order for your customer to understand this high level of skill and commitment, your branding and marketing, of those high standards and skills, is key.

Time for a reminder that you are aiming to work less for more in your cake business, in order to deliver on your goal of running a successful cake business and living the lifestyle you want.

Firstly you should never 'ask the audiences' on Facebook for a price on your cake.

There are regional differences, and your operating costs will be totally different to another cake maker, and so will your profit margins.

Your ultimate dream and goal of the type of lifestyle you want to achieve by running a successful cake business will be different too.

They may not be hunting in their ' happy hunting ground', and therefore they may not have attracted the ideal cake customer, so please don't ask or compare your cake to theirs, as the elements that are involved in cake pricing are more involved than just the fact that there cake looks like yours.

Being the cheapest cake provider in your chosen area isn't sustainable, and how long before someone else joins in and finds a few more efficiencies and undercuts you.

Another word of warning, don't enter the cake business world with a cut price attitude either, just to get you established, as it will come back to haunt you.

I will admit that the cake Facebook groups are beginning to change and the posts are getting better in relation to pricing.

There are still a few new cake businesses owners joining though and still repeating the same old question.

(Take a look at the cake Facebooks groups as they are very supportive generally and full of good ideas).

So you are not providing cakes for the person who selects their cakes according to the price. You are making cakes for those who recognise individuality, skill, and talent.

So keep all the above in mind when you produce your cake pricing strategy.

There are three pricing methods I learned all those years ago.

Three times cost method
Cost + Op Cost + Profit
Cost + Hours of Work+ Op Cost+ Profit (CHOP)

With all of the above methods, you can create a pricing guide for yourself to refer to quickly and easily.

With all these methods confidence is key. If you have taken on board everything I have said in previous chapters, you should have this is mastered by now, if not maybe reread these chapters and it will make cake pricing easier if you have the confidence and belief in yourself.

Method 3 is my preferred pricing method for successful cake businesses. I call it my CHOP method ™.

So here it is my attempt on paper at explaining it.

Pricing cakes using CHOP method

Cake Costs + Hours of Work + Operating Costs + Profit (CHOP Method) ™

Cake Costs

All the ingredients, the boards, the boxes, the ribbons, a teaspoon of vanilla extract, and a teaspoon of baking powder has a cost. Work out your ingredient/material costs and make a spreadsheet of your costs.

Don't forget to revisit these costs regularly, as they can go up quickly and you not notice. Take butter for example which is now nearly 100% dearer than it was a few years ago.

Hours of Work

You need to earn a wage from your business, and in time you may need an assistant or two, and that is another wage to consider.

Many who start a cake business are replacing a wage or an income or working part-time in their own cake business until they can fully replace a full time income, so wages are important and must be thought of as separate from everything else. Your wages are measured in hours.

Work out how long it takes to make your cake or cakes. These are hours actually working on your cake, time when you cannot do any other task, so cakes cooking in the oven doesn't count!

Don't forget to start with the time it takes to design, quote, create an invoice and possibly source products/ingredients that you do not hold in stock.

Also at the other end of the cake making is the cleaning up. Washing up or loading the dishwasher. It's all time when you cannot do anything else.

Once you have a figure for how long a cake will take you, from start to finish, you can put a value on the "Hours of Work in terms of how much you want to earn.

(I have not included the time taken to deliver a cake as a 'Delivery Charge' is a whole different calculation which I will deal with later)

For the sake of giving an example, I will choose to pay myself £20 hour. This is a price plucked out of the air, and by no means is it a guide to paying yourself, as only you know your worth, but your goal is to continually increase your hours of work cost and your profit margin.

Operating Costs

If you have retail premises, a business unit, or you are a home based cake business you will have operating costs.

You need a telephone to take orders, and Wi-Fi to use the internet for social media, emails etc. You may be printing invoices and or leaflets, and therefore using paper and printer ink.

You will have to have public liability insurance, washing up liquid and or dishwasher tablets, cleaning fluids and kitchen roll, the list is exhaustive. Electricity, water and gas, it costs money to operate your cake business. All of these and more are your cake business operating costs.

Marketing your cake business has a cost. You will need to set a marketing budget right from day one and stick to it, but include it in your operating costs. Your marketing budget is an operating cost. I always suggest a marketing budget of £10 month to my new cake business coaching clients to focus them. They soon change it!

You may have taken a loan to buy your equipment or to convert your Kitchen. The loan is also an operating cost. (You may already have your big ticket items like a food mixer, and a laptop computer or tablet, but you can sell these to your new cake business to offset against tax. Make sure you read Chapter 2 for an explanation of how to do this. You will be missing out and losing money if you don't!)

It is best to consult with an expert in relation to tax and expenses. A good accountant is worth his or her weight in gold, when it comes to cake business operating costs and with your tax return.

The rules about what you can and can't claim for in a cake business in relation to tax aren't difficult, but there are quite a few, so best to take some advice which most accountants will give for free hopefully. I know Laura from Smart Online Accountants has lots of advice.

Once you have a yearly 'operating cost', divide this cost by the number of weeks you will expect to work a year.

To do this take away the number of weeks you will expect to take off during your annual summer holidays and your holidays with your loved ones.

Don't forget there are 52 weeks in the year!

You may not be going anywhere on holiday this year, but you just build in time away from your cake business, to ensure you have a good work-life balance.

Example:

Yearly Operating Costs = £ 2000

5 Weeks Holiday / No Cake Business Work Weeks a year.

Therefore you are planning to work 47 weeks in a year in your cake business.

Therefore your weekly 'Operating Costs' is 47 weeks divided £2000.

Therefore your weekly Operating Cost £42.55 (These figures are for demonstration purposes only)

Next, you need to decide on your hours of work in those weeks.

Say you are going to work 40 hours a week in your cake business. You may only have about half of this time to actually work on your cakes and earn an income from them, especially if you are just starting out.

The other 20 hours that week will be the admin, social media, delivering leaflets, holding cake consultations etc., unless you outsource right from the start and build the cost of that outsourcing into your operating costs.

Therefore you have 20 hours on average per week to earn your operating costs by selling your cakes.

So remember we needed £42.55 a week to cover our Operating Costs therefore, but we only have 20 hours to make cakes to earn those costs.

£42.55 divided by 20 hours = £2.12 hour Operating Cost £2.12 hour.

It is a good idea to create an Operating Costs Spreadsheet to ensure you are generating your operating cost every week.

You may only have one cake order one week taking 7 hours in total to complete. This will be a shortfall of 13 hours where you won't be earning your operating costs. What do you do?

Firstly you must make yourself aware of it, and decide whether to carry over the 13hrs x £2.12 = £27.56, to the next week or next month and recalculate the operating costs per hour for that month or week.

Or you could add it to the total operating costs revenue needed in a year and then divide that figure by the number of working weeks and hours you have left.

We aren't running a charity, we are running a business and it is essential that we keep an eye on our cake operating costs. Again the above is an example and is by no means an industry standard.

Profit

There are many reasons to add profit onto the cake cost. Profit allows your cake business to grow by giving you paid development time within your cake business. You need to be paid whilst you develop new cake lines, visit the trade shows, or enter a cake competition to enhance your profile, replace that worn out mixer after a hard year, give you a ' buffer wage' during quiet periods or sickness leave.

There are many more reasons ....

You are also not going to be busy 12 months of the year as cakes, particularly wedding cakes are seasonal so you need to factor in your quiet periods.

There might be periods where you may not be earning a wage as your cake order book is quiet, but you still having to pay operating costs like insurances and web hosting and outsourced functions maybe like social media and accountancy.

You should set a profit margin for your cake business that you are comfortable with.

I suggest that a 20 % profit margin is a good starting point, but this must be revisited regularly, and even as often as after each cake until it can be raised as high as possible. Don't be afraid to push up your profit margin.

So to work out the cost of your profit add up your Ingredient/material costs, hours of work(wage), and operating costs and come to a figure for your cake. Then times this figure by your profit margin %.

So let's put this CHOP ™ cake pricing method together for a ' One Tier Novelty Cake' quote:

Costs = £15
Hours of Work = 3.5 hours
My Wage = £20 ph. Profit Margin = 20%
Op Cost = £2.12 ph.

Apply the CHOP™ method.

Cost + (Hours Work) + (Operating Costs) + (Profit)

£15 + (3.5 x £20) + (3.5 x £2.12) = £70

20 % of £70 is £14

Therefore the cost of this One Tier Novelty Cake is £84.

Delivering Cakes Charge

Please note that I haven't included delivering a cake, particularly a wedding cake, in the cost of the cake above. This is because a delivery charge is a separate calculation.

Yes, you will charge your time whilst you are driving, delivering and setting up. You are after all away from your 'cake factory' and you are not making other cakes and earning money.

Yes, you will include mileage, on top of your time.

You can base your mileage on the government rate of 45p a mile (This is what you can claim in tax terms and covers fuel and wear and tear on your vehicle).

Example: Delivering a cake 5 miles away.

The journey there and back and hand over 1hr.

Hours of work 1 x £20

Mileage 10 x 45p

Delivery charge £24.50

This is actually your worth if you want to pay yourself £20. Even if you paid yourself the minimum wage in your business, £7.83 *, your delivery charge would be £12.53!

Use your time wisely and take a look at whether or not you will be delivering your cakes or using a cheaper more cost effective way like a courier or an assistant (maybe in the future).

A quick note about wedding cake deliveries here. I always deliver my wedding cakes and charge a 'set up fee' too in terms of hours of work.

From experience, there were always at least two of us on a wedding cake delivery and set up. I also used to assist other wedding cake makers with their setups so a little reminder to charge your assistants time too per hour including their travelling.

Wholesale Cake Prices

Now let's talk about wholesale prices. If you have decided to sell your cakes to local cafes and shops, then you will need to find your formula for wholesale selling of your cakes.

Let's take for example a box of 12 cupcakes.

By batch cooking my cupcakes I can make and bake 48 cupcakes in the same time I can make and bake 12. (One large batter mix, and four trays in my oven at a time. My 1kg of butter icing normally covers the 48 cupcakes.)

Therefore using the CHOP™ method we used before, the ingredient cost will be higher with 48 cupcakes, but the hours of work and operating costs will be the same as for 12.

Therefore I would make my minimum order 48 cupcakes for wholesale cupcakes. (Again this is my example in order to illustrate a point.)

Friends and Family

So your friends and family have been your biggest supporters, having spurred you on into your dream cake business when you were a hobby caker, but now you are a cake business owner, and have set working hours in order to earn enough money to realise your goals of living your ideal lifestyle. So it's time to think like a business owner and manage their expectations whilst not forgetting their part in your journey. Don't forget they could become barrier to your success.

My best advice is to talk to them before they give you that last minute call for a two tier cake for a very special occasion. Planning is key here. You can put special big occasions on your planner, before you are asked, and offer to make the cake in advance, rather than wait until the last minute.

You could choose not to charge for your cake as it's your gift, or you could charge for the ingredients. Only you know the relationship you have with your friends and family. It is a great opportunity especially if there is a party to get your name out there, with all your relatives sharing pictures of your cake on social media. It is also a chance to get some product development in with the bonus of having all the ingredients and maybe some of your time paid for.

Handle them with care.

Discounts

There may be an outer layer of friends or acquaintances who are contacting you as you may have offered them a discount in the past.

You may be planning your wedding fares and for those that book a wedding cake consultation at the event, there may be a discount. There are lots of occasions where discounts get you that lifelong cake customer.

I know the business and pricing models of well-known large businesses in the UK are based on their discounted or sale price.

From clothing to furniture, we see them have at least four big sales a year. Reality is that the sale price and units sold is their actual target and the non-sale price is a bonus.

So where can you make the savings in order to give this discount? Your ingredients/material costs are what they are, and you still need to cover your wage and operating costs so the only variable is your profit margin.

Therefore ensure that your profit margin is healthy enough to withstand the occasional discount. Remember our profit margins aren't a luxury, they are necessary for cake business success.

Competitor Analysis

I mentioned not comparing yourself to other cake businesses, in previous chapters, but the correct competitor analysis is very important

It is important to understand right from the get-go that it is almost unheard of for any business, let alone a cake business, to not have a competitor. A real competitor!

A real competitor is another cake business in the top 20% of cake businesses above the waterline as described in chapter 1.

Never consider the cheap cake person or hobby caker in your area to be your competitor. They are serving the group of cake customers who are cheap cake hunters and are not your ideal cake customers, so do not worry about them

It is important to understand right from the get-go that it is almost unheard of for any business, let alone a cake business, to not have a real competitor. It is equally important right from day one that you identify who they are and develop your cake business to be different, unique and of course better than theirs.

Look at their website, their social media and see if you can define their niche, their brand, and their unique selling point if they have one.

What I will say, which is quite unique to the cake business, is quite often these real cake competitors become your 'professional allies'. I stopped short of saying 'friend' there, as there are no friends in business, but there are allies, collaborators, and affiliates.

It seems harsh, but that mind set helped me so much in the cake business and business in general, and made me a better person and business woman.

So if you do find a real cake competitor in your chosen area you will need to carry out a cake competitor analysis exercise. (I have outlined how to do this below.)

Don't worry it's painless, interesting and very easy to do. It won't take you long and doesn't mean you have to be a scientist either. Bear with me, as it is vital to your cake business success.

It may be that their customer service isn't as hot as yours in their telephone manner, answer phone, texts or emails or even their social media presence.

Your cake offerings may be very unique and different to your real cake competitors. You may offer a completely different range of cakes, styles, and colour palettes, or you understand and promote gluten, vegan or alcohol-free cakes.

Now I'm not suggesting here that you try the mystery cake customer approach, to test their level of customer service, as it becomes fairly obvious when the shoe is on the other foot. It is very annoying when it is you who is on the receiving end of a competitor doing their own cake business analysis, so don't do it.

This cake competitor may not be meeting a need in that area or meeting it but their customer service is poor.

By meeting a need, I mean maybe not providing gluten, or dairy free or eggless. Or you know they do cater for it, but they aren't promoting that they do.

Check the top 50 cake businesses list on Google. Do you have one of these cake businesses in your chosen cake selling area?

Ask at hotels and wedding venues who usually supplies the wedding cakes.

Visit the wedding fairs and take a look.

Look on Yell.com and Freeindex for cake suppliers in your chosen area.

Type 'Cake suppliers nearby' into a Google search whilst in your chosen area. Your phone will automatically go to 'near me' so be careful as you may not live in or near your chosen cake selling area.

Get to know the people on Facebook / Instagram / Twitter / Pinterest. Use #cake #birmingham to find them on social media.

If they have a physical shop maybe go in and introduce yourself ..... madness I know but it works.

Be careful to ensure that they are comparable to your cake business, real competitors.

Real cake competitors are not to be looked upon in a negative way. It is quite common for fellow cake business owners to recognise their competitor's high standards and services. I certainly saw this happen with referrals from other real cake competitors when they were too busy.

So now that you have identified them get to know their offerings, tastes, and services. Take a look at their pricing structure as a matter of interest but never compare.

Your ideal cake customer will come to you because of your style, your brand, your values, your customer service, lots of reasons but I am sure price will not come into it for most.

Use their pricing as a benchmark perhaps if you are just starting out in that area, but do not undercut their prices, as this strategy has repercussions and evokes bad feelings.

You may want to offer cakes in a similar price range as a newbie into what may be seen as their area, but never undercut, add value to your service when initially starting out in this new area.

Offer something the ideal cake customer values, which may not have a high-cost implication to you, but they value, in order to get your foot in the door.

Maybe you are launching in a new area and its near to Valentines or Mother's Day.

Maybe offer a free hand-tied bouquet of flowers, with every cake ordered for these dates as a special promotion.

I did this once. I went to my local Lidl and selected a £3 beautiful bunch of flowers. I did, in fact, grab as many as I had cake orders for and I wrapped them in a beautiful tissue I found at a local market and tied them up with a hessian bow and a luggage tag with my cake business name on.

They looked really expensive and cost me £4.50 at most.

Work on this price as you could align yourself with a local florist who is prepared to do this for you, at a similar cost and put your poster and leaflet to in their shop. You could cross promote each other. Collaboration is key remember.

Don't forget that this real cake competitor analysis isn't a one-off, you need to do this regularly.

"In business, the competition will bite you if you keep running, if you stand still they will swallow you" - Victor Kiam CEO Remmington

As mentioned previously, do not be tempted to copy another person's cake. Enough said!

Having Confidence to Hold a Pricing Conversation

Now you have a pricing structure for your cake business, and you are clear on what you want to earn, your operating costs and your profit margins, it is time to look at the confidence to name your price.

This is another area where some of my cake business students and clients have difficulty with their cake businesses.

Having taken on board and understood that a good pricing structure with a healthy profit margin, will deliver them a successful cake business, delivering on their goals and vision they then stumble at the prospect of publishing their prices.

Even saying those prices out loud on the telephone or in a cake consultation fills them with fear.

I have been there, and this is not something that will disappear immediately, overnight. This confidence to name your cake price is something that needs to be worked on,
and maybe an issue in your deep subconscious.

It is not unusual for any successful businessman, or woman, to work on their 'mindset', with a mindset coach to give them confidence to believe in themselves, their abilities, and their prices. I will admit that I have had my own mindset coach in the past.

The way I coach my clients, my Cakepreneurs, relies heavily on mindset coaching in order to achieve the successful cake business that they deserve.

So the key is to believe in yourself and your cakes and to transmit this belief to your ideal cake customer. You will eventually shake off the cheeky ones, who ask how much for a cake, and when you tell them they huff and puff, and say you are too expensive, and that they can get one for half the price!

These are not your ideal customer so don't worry about them.

Hopefully, your targeted marketing will be so good and in the right areas to the right ideal customers, that you won't attract these cheap cake hunters. We have all had them but I'm happy to say it's a thing of the past for me.

I do despair when I read the stories posted nearly every day by members of some Facebook groups by cake business owners. Their experience of cheap cake hunters makes my toes curl, as I remember those days.

So how do you stop being a magnet for the cheap cakes hunters? Here are my top ten tips

1. Don't look like a cheap cake provider! Ensure your cakes are photographed well and pay a little to get your cake range photographed professionally.

2. Stay on brand and make sure your brand says professional. Invest time in learning and developing your brand.

3. Have a clear and concise pricing strategy with a profit margin. If you research many of the Top 50 cake businesses in the UK you will see that they do actually price their cakes on their website, so don't be afraid to do the same.

4. When taking a cake enquiry over the phone, after introducing yourself and asking 'How can I help you today?' I always ask them what their budget was if it wasn't a wedding cake. Now if they are a cheap cake hunter you will know straight away as they will give one .From my experience ideal cake customers

don't have a set budget. Your time is precious and you can't afford to waste it so at this point you have a decision to make

Do you finish the call quite quickly, but politely or do you continue and sell your brand, your uniqueness, and your professionalism. In a well-rehearsed speech, that doesn't have to last too long but remember every contact counts, and on this occasion it may be a cheap cake they require, but on the next occasion they may have promoted themselves to your ideal cake customer. Remember the film 'Pretty Woman!'

Thank them for their enquiry and ask if they have looked at your website. Give them a flavour of you and your unique selling points before stating that your celebration cakes start from x amount of pounds for a two layer 6-inch cake.

This conversation should end with them wishing they could afford one of your cakes and making the dream of ordering one an aspirational thing for their future celebrations.

It should not end with you having sold your soul, and becoming a cheap cake supplier or discounting your cake heavily to reach their ridiculously low budget.

5. Make sure your website or Facebook page has recent testimonials on it preferably, with the cake they ordered on show too.

6. Always answer the phone in a professional and courteous manner let's get this conversation off to a great start immediately.

7. Quickly develop a rapport with the customer. Never forget people buy people. I will never forget a well-known local

furniture store near to where I lived. They had a sales lady who was
amazing and outsold everyone else. When a customer enquired about a particular sofa she was always quick to tell them that they had perfect taste as she had this exact same sofa at home!

Now I'm not saying she was being economical with the truth, but if that was the case, she must have lived in a mansion as I had heard her say over the past few weeks that she had nearly all of the sofas in the store!

I am not advocating any untruths here, but I am just outlining how one particular saleswoman worked. I believe that you should be truthful and tell them about your popular cakes and why people say they are delicious, and maybe direct the customer to your reviews on your website or Facebook page. The bottom line is to build a rapport with the customer when holding that pricing conversation.

I will discuss a strategy for holding a pricing conversation at a wedding consultation in the next section of this chapter.

One big element of working on your mindset to achieve your cake business success is celebrating your 'wins'. Celebrate your achievement in landing that big cake order, or high ticket wedding cakes with accompanying desert table order. These are wins and you should celebrate them.

Actually, take time to give yourself a pat on the back and announce to your cakey friends in your Facebook groups or to your family. Give yourself a big YES! and a high five!

<u>Wedding Cake Consultations</u>

I have been teaching how to hold wedding cake consultations for nearly 6 years now, and nothing changes.

Wedding cakes styles come and go, but it never alters that this is a big occasion for the happy couple, and is a major part in the lead up to the wedding.

As I said I have had 5 wedding invitations for this year, so weddings are certainly not going out of fashion.

Having had many more friends venture down this path, over the past few years, I can say without any doubt that they all know the saying.

"If you want anything for a wedding, put a few noughts on the end!"

But they have all ended up having exactly what they wanted, and sod the price, as far as wedding dresses, wedding cakes and venues were concerned. It is a special day after all.

They want what they want, and they will have it no matter the cost.

So as a cake business, give them what they want, and if they don't know what they want, then show them. Make this a special occasion for them and stand out from your competitors by making it so.

What they want is your high-end bespoke wedding cake, unique to them, handcrafted, with the delicious signature buttercreams maybe, designed by a sugar craft artist, you!

Now don't panic if you haven't started your cake business yet if the words 'sugar craft artist' worries you. You can become competent in all aspects of sugar craft in a very short time either by attending a class or learning online or in magazines like Cake Masters.

I have been teaching cake decorating for many years and the results that my students are getting from just a few of our cake decorating classes with myself, Jo and the team are amazing.

You may already be very skilled in all, or most, aspects of sugar craft, making flowers, modelling, royal icing etc., so don't be afraid to use this term if you have the skills.

If it hasn't dawned on you yet then the high-end wedding cake market is the most profitable end of any cake business, and a market you seriously need to explore on your journey to cake business success.

I was mentoring one of my 'Cakepreneurs' the other day, and she had set up a cake business making celebration cakes etc., and wondered why her wedding cakes weren't commanding the prices she needed, or the fact that she was getting very few enquiries. I will disguise her details but she had named her cake business Nanny Bakes (Not the real name).

(This was her first consultation with me.)

I immediately looked at her website and Facebook page and saw that she was displaying lots of her lovely character celebration cakes alongside the odd wedding cake. Her work was excellent and well presented, but it was a mix of prices, colours, and styles.

She was doing quite well building the celebration cake part of her business, but she had clear aspirations to get more high-end wedding cake orders.

I soon pointed out that her branding, her business name and the pictures of her excellent birthday cakes did not say high-end wedding cake artist unfortunately.

(I am passionate about helping people to start or grow a successful cake business, but I will say what I see when asked for help and guidance!)

The solution was simple. Either she rebranded totally, and concentrated solely on the wedding cake business, or she kept her successful celebration cake business and added a new cake business, with a new name and brand to launch or relaunch her into the high-end wedding cake business. She took the latter option and is planning her launch as I write this book.

Another one of my cake business clients, whom I mentor, was complaining about her recent appearances at wedding fairs!

Now I can't hide my dislike of wedding fairs, as a marketing budget spend, not only in time and money, but hey ho, she had booked these fairs a while back, and was committed to appearing.

Her complaint was that the events were saturated with wedding cake makers, who were all of a high standard, and had cakes not dissimilar to hers, and in the same price range .She had found her cake competition. Sound familiar?

I advised her to change her cake style, and go with something original and conceptual maybe. I advised her to get hold of the wedding magazines and research next year's colours and develop a new cake theme perhaps.

I also gave her lots of other advice, which would fill half of this book, but you will find other suggestions as you read on.

Don't be afraid to push the envelope.

Maybe keep yourself to one medium like chocolate. There is a wedding cake designer in the Midlands renowned for his chocolate wrap wedding cakes!

Once you find yourself with the herd, other cake competitors, in your happy hunting ground, take a look at all aspects of your cake business to differentiate yourself from them.

Another one of my Cakepreneurs, after attending a few wedding fairs, realised that there was a big demand for wedding cakes amongst the Asian community in her area , and in particular eggless cakes. This was a hidden community that she had not considered targeting before for her wedding cakes.

I was so proud of her when she told me she was now concentrating on the eggless wedding cake market, and that she had taken advice and learned lots about her new customer base, her new ideal customer, in their likes and styles.

Never be afraid to change course to a destination you never knew existed when you first set out.

So let's talk about the wedding cake consultations as this is your chance to land that big cake order.

Do you hold them at home, amongst the washing on the radiators and the kids popping in for a drink of water?

This was my big issue when I first started out on my cake business journey, and I resolved it by carrying out my consultations in the lounge area of a very nice hotel nearby, which was a very upmarket wedding venue in itself.

The price of using this quiet lounge, or on occasion private room, well it cost the price of four cups of tea purchased from the bar.

You may know of another location that suits you better than your own home, but never be afraid to think outside of the cake box.

Eventually, when I moved house, I deliberately decorated my dining room in a sympathetic style to complement my cake brand, and I had display cabinets, which I bought from Ikea, to display my fabulous showstopper wedding cakes in. The children were a bit older then and were as quiet as church mice when I held a cake consultation.

I prepared my sample cakes in advance, batch cooking and freezing them in finger-size portions. I took them out of the freezer on the morning of the consultation and displayed them on white plates, with a little flag stating what they were. I did the same with the flavoured buttercreams.

The smell of baking always filled the house when my wedding consultation clients arrived, which set the scene.

Had I made a cake for the occasion, no, I had taken out a bunch of cake offcuts, that I always freeze, which were left over from levelling my cakes, and put the frozen remains in the oven on 150 c to produce an effective aroma 15 minutes before the wedding couple arrived.

Note maybe turn the oven down during the consultation as the smell of burning can be quite off- putting. Lesson learned early on!

Now, when they were settled the sofa, with a small complementary soft drink and ready for the star of the show, my leather-bound wedding cake photo album appeared.

You know the sort, you just can't help buying it when you see it. The one with the paper in between each picture.

I would hand over the album to the bride/groom like it was the Holy Grail, from one of the Indiana Jones films, and I watched as they turned to the first picture, which was always my showstopper wedding cake (It also happens to be my most expensive cake, funny that!)

As they viewed my showstopper wedding cake, I made their mouths water by describing the luscious buttercream fillings that make up the layers, and I detailed the sugar craft work that adorned it.

I described my showstopper as a one-off, which would be tailored to their own bespoke design, and that no one else would ever have this same cake, it would be unique.

(Now, sometimes the wedding party would come to the consultation with specific ideas of what they would want their wedding cake to look like and I would be guided by this, but it would never be an exact copy !.

I would then let them look through the rest of the cake album, from my show stopper backwards to my least expensive cake, and when they had finished, and only then, did I offer a tasting of the samples.

I would then ask which cake the decision maker liked, it was usually the bride, although I did have a few grooms with definite ideas of exactly what they wanted.

I would then congratulate him or her their good taste, as more often than not they had chosen the first showstopper wedding cake.

I only mentioned the cost when they asked for the price. I would then write down the sizes and flavours of their wedding cakes and the specifics of the design, before referring to the pricing menu that I had in my folder.

I would then give them the price for their wedding cake.

Eventually, when I expanded my cake range I would ask if they were having a dessert table, as the price for the desert table usually brings the price of the wedding cake down.

I did, of course, have examples of dessert tables I could supply, with a combined price for the dessert table with the wedding cake.

Another consideration is wedding favours which you could include in a package price with the wedding cake.

Now the price you are giving the customer, for the wedding cake, is for you to make the wedding cake only. I usually ask the customer if they want the delivery and set up service too. This is an additional cost don't forget!

A quick note about delivery and set up charges.

Find out the exact location of the wedding and use google maps to find out the number of miles and the time it takes to travel there and back.

(I never do a wedding cake delivery and set up alone, as two pairs of hands are always needed. Even if it is your partner or a friend, take someone, and remember that the spare pair of hands will need paying!)

Mileage is usually at least 45p a mile or your own mileage rate, and your time includes traveling there and back and set up.

I always allow at least an hour set up, even with the simplest cake, as I find that you can be hanging about waiting to given access to the venue room, or waiting for someone to sign off the hand over the document at the venue.

Finally always take a payment for your cake consultation before the event, which can be redeemed against the cost of the wedding cake if you want too. You are providing a service and you have charges.

If your hourly rate is £20 charge that together with your operating costs at least.

I always limited my wedding cake consultations to an hour and I made sure the couple knew this beforehand, in order to manage their expectations.

I didn't in the early days and as most of my consultations were in the evening at home. I wondered, on one occasion, how I was going to get the wedding cake customers out of my house, after two hours, as one couple seemed to be settled in for the night!

Always take a non-refundable deposit there and then, for the wedding cake order, before they leave, as you are getting heavily booked up.

Have a deposit disclaimer on your website or Facebook page, for the customer to refer too.

A 50 % non-refundable deposit is not unusual. I will have a copy of a 'wedding cake deposit disclaimer' on my website for you to refer to, but having it printed out and signed by the happy couple at the consultation, is even better.

It is a non-refundable deposit!

Finally, limit the number of people attending the wedding cake consultation as some people regard it as an evening out, and a feeding frenzy and you do find the more people there, the more confused the decision maker gets.

Full payment for the wedding cake is normally 4 weeks ahead of the date. I made it 6 weeks personally.

Chapter 6: Marketing Offline

Why it is Important

I truly believe that a successful cake business is 20% about how good your cakes are, and 80% marketing. The caveat here though "is you can't polish a poo", or the cake equivalent.

Therefore I place such high importance on marketing that I have decided to split marketing into two chapters, offline (not on the internet) in this chapter, and online in chapter 7.

Now, marketing your cake business is a very serious science, and I could fill a whole book on the subject, but I will try and break it down to what is really important.

My basic theory (It possibly belongs to someone else way back and got embedded in my head) is simple. Marketing is buying customers!

Once you understand this basic theory, it may help you make marketing decisions, particularly marketing spend decisions, in your cake business far more effectively.

Let me explain.

For example, if you pay for a Facebook advert costing £100, and this advert brings you four paying cake customers, each cake customer has cost you £25 to buy!

Don't worry this is only an example, and once you have purchased your cake customer, they will usually come on a journey with you as their cake supplier, and this investment of £25 may secure you a number of cake orders from them.

If you value your relationship with this cake customer, they may tell their friends and family what a great cake you made for them, and what excellent customer service you gave, and that £25 investment in this cake customer may go even further than you think.

I find that I always treated a cake customer as a precious purchase for my cake business and I looked after my relationship with them.

For example, perhaps they ordered a birthday cake from you for their daughter's birthday on the10th February. Well, that birthday isn't going to change year after year, so how about popping the date in your diary and maybe six weeks ahead of time, next year, email Mom your new ideas and cake range.

Always worth writing on a calendar on the wall, or electronically, the reason for the cake order and customer who ordered a cake, and use it as a handy reference the following year. Think ahead and set an alert to pop up six weeks before. Use technology.

Maybe a season's greeting card too, always says they are valued. Try and hand write it.

I know it's silly but I get one each year from an Indian takeaway we used occasionally, but since receiving their Christmas card, I feel as though I must use them on a Friday night as they value me! Seems silly, but it works on me.

If you get 500 leaflets printed at a cost of £100 and post them out and get 5 cake orders from the leaflet campaign, again you have a cost of buying each customer for £20. Be careful though that the time taken to post through letterboxes is has a cost of you not working directly in your business.

I once knew a cake maker who regularly advertised her elegant couture wedding cakes week after week, in a local newspaper costing her £60 a week.

When I asked her how many customers she had got from this advert she said she was unsure.

Unsure, she actually didn't know where her cake customers came from. It is as simple as asking when the customer contacts you and make a note.

If none of her customers were as a result of this newspaper advert then she was wasting her money.

This act of buying customers need not be seen as a negative thing. It can also be seen as an investment too. You could be investing £60 to bring about £180 worth of cake orders. But if you don't know if your investment paid off how will you know.

The only other thing you need to know about marketing, is the customers are buying you too!

Two great ladies, Abigail Horne and Sarah Stone from the Female Success Network talk about heart to heart 'H2H 'marketing. They may not have created the acronym, but it's a great one for focusing the mind when marketing.

www.femalesuccessnetwork.com.

Your cake customers need to connect with you as your brand, and as the fabulous creative cake person that you are. That is why the branding and naming of your business is so important.

There is a lot of what I say in this book and to my cake business students, my Cakepreneurs, about marketing, that is true for both offline and online marketing of your cake business

Take, or have taken, good pictures of your cakes, and spend some time and a bit of money in getting them right. Have a brand background colour which is clearly identified as your cake brands picture, and get the lighting right. You don't have to get every cake photographed just your statement showstopper cakes

These pictures will stand you in a great place for years, believe me.

Finally, I want you to understand that marketing your cake business, is not about trying to force people to buy your cakes or products, it's about showing potential customers that you are different, you have a clear brand and identity and that you are the bee's knees. Your cakes are lovingly created and not thrown together in a factory.

That reminds me, I had to stop the car the other day as I heard a radio advert which stopped me in my tracks.

The advert was for a coffee shop (I think), as it was so ridiculous I didn't concentrate on the name or where it was.

The advert said it's barista's "lovely served handcrafted coffee" in their shop!

Well how ridiculous, I thought, as I'm sure food hygiene regulations would prevent them doing it with their feet, and how on earth would they make and serve a coffee if it wasn't with their hands.

I think you understand what I'm getting at, but this advert had overstepped the mark in my mind with its poetic license trying to sell cups of coffee, and turned itself into pure desperate comedy. That's my view and personal to me though. So be real with your marketing.

Market your strengths, market you and your high standards, market your friendly approachable personality and your smile.

So let's delve a little deeper into marketing offline.

From day one when you start your cake business, you will get calls offering you all these wild and wonderful marketing deals. If you have been running your cake business for a while you will know exactly what I'm talking about.

Don't get me wrong I have fallen into the trap of having a so called fabulous advert in some magazine, which was to be given free of charge to every customer of a high-end supermarket in my target area, my happy hunting ground. It sounded an amazing opportunity that I couldn't miss.

This was the right demographic for me, and wrongly I jumped at the chance and spent a small fortune.

I didn't have any concept of a marketing budget for my cake business at the time, and I certainly wasn't evaluating the effectiveness of my marketing spend on a monthly basis.

So I paid for the advert in this glossy magazine and needless to say, I did visit the supermarket in order to see every customer thumbing through the magazine and seeing my advert. Wrong!

I eventually found the magazine with my advert in, piled up in a sad looking 'help yourself' type box against the wall behind the pet food donation bin, gathering dust.

Big lesson learned, but oh no, I did it again, I took an unsolicited call and paid for an advert in another magazine which was to be given out at one of the cake industry's top shows.

Once again no sign of the magazine at the show until another help yourself box was found at the back of the hall.

You can understand I didn't get any orders from these adverts I just lost a lot of money. My advice, avoid these offers like the plague!!!!!!

When you get the call, they will build you up. They will say you have been chosen as the only cake business in the area etc... Well stop them there.

My rule is now that if I want to spend my marketing budget with you the advertiser, I will be calling you, and not the other way around. I do turn the conversation around now and offer to sell them a cake though.

You will have included a marketing budget in your cake business operating costs, per month, already and you will know how much money, if any, you are willing to allocate from your marketing budget per month to a particular advertising venture.

Advertising and Wedding Fairs

One way of getting the word out and marketing your cake business is wedding fairs.

Wedding fairs are generally hosted from January to March and then again in September to October, and are a way of being personal and interacting with your ideal cake customers.

But do your homework and vet the wedding fairs first. Maybe go along with a friend and speak to a few other exhibitors and see how they have found it. Have a chat with the organiser and look around. Is it busy with brides, and is it well signposted?

Will the organiser be capturing contact details of those attending and where will they be publicising the event and how many attended last time they held one? Always good questions for the organiser to answer.

How many real cake competitors are there, and what types of cakes are they selling etc.

There is usually a cost implication to having a stand at a wedding fair so be prepared. This is a marketing budget spend from your operating budget remember.

If you do attend a wedding fair as an exhibitor, maybe run a competition on the day and get the potential ideal cake customers details, their emails and social media details via a 'Goldfish Bowl' type competition.

Maybe offer a free box of cupcakes as a prize for the draw at the end of the day, and make sure you email them later to thank them for their interest and direct them to your website and social media.

Always go to fairs close to your chosen cake selling area, your happy hunting ground, and that you can get to easily when the booking comes through.

Finally, on wedding fairs just a reminder that January - February in the UK can mean snow, and I know as I was caught out once where I had already spent my marketing budget on a wedding fair as an exhibitor and because of the snow no one came! Nope, they are still too much of a gamble for me.

Another good marketing idea is finding local high-end kitchen shops and places like Hobby Craft and Lakeland and offering to do a free cake decorating demonstration, maybe with some of their equipment they have on sale. Collaboration is key I say.

Referrals. Nothing speaks louder than a great recommendation from an ideal cake customer. Maybe mention to your customers if they recommend you to a friend or colleague and the friend or colleague places a cake order (above a certain value) they will get a free box of your delicious cupcakes. Make it a box of six cupcakes tied with a ribbon, and a thank you note. Include business cards in the cake box and ask them to pass onto friends and colleagues.

Stipulate that the customer must live within a certain mile radius of your business as you don't want to incur extra mileage and time away from your business, whilst delivering a free gift after all.

The cost of this seemingly grand gesture is minimal to you in terms of your cake marketing budget, but will be perceived by the customer as a great gesture. If they aren't local maybe they can suggest a recipient who does live nearby.

Try and steer away from giving a discount off their next order though as that's revenue you're losing. Better to add value by giving something that the customer perceives as valuable but actually doesn't cost you that much is key to referrals and retaining customers.

Signs in cars, your car, your partner's car, mom and dad's car etc. If you haven't got a shop window use every space you possibly own, or have access to, to put up a sign, a free advert for your cake business. There are lots of companies that make these signs online, like Vista print etc.

Posters or A4 leaflets are a great idea too. Get one designed and make sure your unique selling points are obvious on there. Maybe include a QR (Quick Response) code on the poster, so that people with smartphones can see your web site straight away. Give these out to friends and relatives to put up in communal areas at their place of work maybe.

Put up a poster campaign. Set yourself a challenge. I set myself this challenge every three months. By poster I mean an A4 flyer designed and made either by yourself using an app like Canva.

Use online companies like Vistaprint or a local company to design one and get it printed.

Your poster needs to be showing at least one of your showstopper cakes. It needs to be in your brand colours and it needs to show all the services you offer and your contact details.

The next step is making a list of all family and friends who are willing to help you and give them as many posters as you can, to put it in kitchens and communal areas at their places of work.

Make it a challenge between them, maybe suggest they put their names as a reference on the poster and reward them, if they need encouraging when you get a referral from that poster.

I find it easy to set myself an actual number of posters I want out there and then find people to put them up. When I run out of family and friendsI then go to my contacts in the local supermarket and stores and ask them to put up in staff rooms and in shop windows. I have even been known to go to big business estates and bribe the receptionists with a few gorgeous cupcakes, for the office, and ask her to put them up in the canteen or canteens.

Warning. Don't let the posters go sour and out of date. Remember to renew them in November and at the end of January ready for Christmas, Valentines and Mother's Day respectively.

More Great Marketing Ideas

There are many ways to get your business noticed and to find your ideal cake customers

How about teaming up with your local wedding industry suppliers. Wedding cakes are your best high ticket sales items.

If you know me well you will know that I always advocate that the wedding cake market is the market you should be in.

I know I have said this before and I don't apologise for trying to tempt you down this route in order to be a success in the cake business

Try finding the wedding suppliers in your area, where your ideal cake customer lives, and go and talk to them.

Yes talk, pop in and have a natter. Always a good idea to have a cupcake or six to help the conversation flow a bit better.

Ask the florist or the bridal shop owner if you can display one of your magnificent wedding cake dummies in their window, to complement their dress or floral displays.

They might bite your hand off, as this is an exceptional freebie for them. If not come up with some cross-promotion agreement, with each other to market each other's business. Bottom line ask to rent a space in their window.

I believe heavily in the concept of 'giving back' to a just cause, and as a business, I have always supported a local charity.

In fact, I choose a new charity a year to support. (Then when I get a cold call from other charities I am okay with saying 'no thank you' and that maybe I will consider the other charity next year).

So along those lines, there are many other worthy groups you could choose to support.

I chose the police and the NHS. Both these worthy organisations have sports and social clubs, which have their own intranet pages.

From my own personal knowledge, the employees within these organisations regularly trawl their respective intranet websites for local deals and discounts.

Why not contact the respective sports and social clubs from these or other organisations like these, and offer a discount to their staff off their first cake orders, and other little incentives to show your appreciation of their work.

Don't forget you are a business and not a charity and maybe reread the discount section in Chapter 5.

The advert on these sports and social club sites were free.

Now, I'm not saying that these two organisations are the only ones deserving of your special discount, as I have left out the fire and ambulance service, but you get the idea.

I have mentioned the adverts in the back of the car, but I also find that the lovely big sign I used to display in my rear window, when delivering and setting up wedding cakes, which said "wedding cake delivery in progress" got lots of attention when I left it in the rear window for a week or so .

A branded fleece coat for you and your partner. If you don't ask you don't get!

Even having your hair done it's a great marketing opportunity. This may be a treat booking yourself in to have your hair done, be careful to choose the right salon in the right area where your ideal customer would use.

Let's face it hair salons are where we hear lots of hints and tips and advice, as well as a fair deal of local gossip. But one thing hairdressers are good at and that's recommending their customers.

If you don't have a hairdresser it may be worth finding one for a quick blow dry and spread the word about your fabulous cake business in your chosen cake selling area.

Don't forget that the male members of your family. They use the barbers and this is a great place to put leaflets and posters in the run-up to the Valentines and Mother's Day, all for the price of a few cupcakes usually.

My favourite marketing idea was the summer and Christmas fairs at the schools in my ideal customer area. I loved these marketing occasions.

I also love the village or school fete for getting my name and my cakes out there.

I would suggest that you use these as a PR marketing occasions with a great display of your dummy cakes and maybe a few nibbles to give away. Make sure you're in your cake decorating whites and looking totally the part.

Attract people to come and talk to you with a few bowls of strategically placed quality street on the front of your table. Ask them to take part in your free raffle draw to win the most gorgeous box of cupcakes tied with a beautiful bow again and lovingly displayed on your table. The 'Goldfish Bowl' draw idea comes out again.

Simply ask the people entering the competition to fill out a pre-prepared slip with their name and telephone number on and of course their email address.

This then gets put into a goldfish bowl. I also ask if they would like to follow my Facebook or other social media page whilst they are there. If they do so, on the spot, I give them another free entry to my prize draw.

The value of this marketing opportunity is amazing in the information you can harvest from the people you meet, and you're able to contact them in the future with your fabulous cake offers. I have had a table at a high and junior school summer fete for as little as a £10 donation to the school.

Finally in this offline marketing section is your business card, seems simple but I bet you haven't done this yet.

Every time I pop to the supermarket to pick up 'cakey' stuff the checkout desk person always asks me "are you making cakes?"

Even walking around the supermarket I was always bumping into mums I knew from the kid's school days, and they would ask "how you are what are you doing". Both of these supermarket interactions are cues to get out your business card.

I've even been guilty of leaving them on the tables at Costa Coffee when I leave. Set yourself a weekly target of how many business cards you can give out a week, expand this number by roping in family and friends too.

I could again fill a book with marketing ideas for your cake business. There are blogs on my website www.thecakebizcoach.com with more great marketing ideas so check them out.

How to Launch or Relaunch Your Cake Business

Holding a launch or a relaunch is a great offline marketing idea.

This is a must whether you are launching at the start of your cake business or have undertaken a rebranding.

Now we are not talking a high budget swanky sparkly occasion, with celebrity openings, and a ribbon cutting ceremony!

I'm sure your home kitchen at home is lovely but unless you are very lucky, you won't be holding a launch event in it, but don't dismiss it straight away.

The launch or relaunch is just putting a label on a date on your cake business calendar in big bold letters, 'LAUNCH', and working towards your 'Project Cake Business Launch/Relaunch', with a clear and concise plan to get you there.

What you will need to keep an eye on is that any spend on this launch will come out of your marketing budget, which sits under your operating costs. Just a reminder this before you get carried away.

If you have followed my suggestion and set your first marketing budget monthly allowance as low as £10 a month, you may have to use three months marketing budget in one go.

(I'm not being mean here, I just wanted you to focus on a figure and I chose £10 as a challenge as your monthly marketing budget!)

It is very doable, if you are creative, so as a business woman or man who is the owner of a bespoke cake company, of course, you will be keeping an eye on the marketing budget.

So why hold a launch event?

Well it gets your cake business out there, and ensures that you at least do something, and set a date and a goal to work to, getting your marketing material ready.

You will never achieve your cake business success goal without planning and deadlines, so a launch or relaunch is a great focuser of the mind.

Here's a simple launch event idea.

Approach a store in the area that you have chosen as your 'Happy Hunting Ground'. One that aligns best to where your ideal customer would shop.

It could be a wedding dress shop, or florists that you have aligned yourself to, or are collaborating with, or a cake decorating equipment supplier like Lakeland or Hobby Craft.

I have worked with both Lakeland and Hobby Craft in the past, and they love the idea of cake decorating demonstrators in their stores, to pull the customers in.

Perhaps pop in and see the manager and negotiate a deal where you demonstrate a few rose swirls on a few cupcakes, maybe using their nozzles, but treat it as your launch, and have your show stopper dummy or dummies cakes on your demo table, with a load of business cards.

(This is just one idea with one eye on the marketing budget, there are many others ideas.)

Engage with people at the event and talk to them about your unique selling points (USP), maybe you put your 5-star food hygiene rating in a frame on the table, and just sell you and your cake business to customers who visit their store.

Try and go on a busy day when the store will be busy. If not, no worries, just ensure you publicise the event and ask the store to do the same. Maybe have the chance to win a box of cupcakes again. The 'Goldfish Bowl' appears again!

At the launch event, you could do a live Facebook broadcast, telling people that you are in the store today for a few hours. Ask people to share your post and pop down to see you, as they could be walking away with a box of delicious cupcakes.

If you have an unusual USP maybe contact the local newspaper, and tell them that you are launching, and give them a human interest story to latch onto.

Newspapers love human interest stories. You may have retired or been made redundant and started your business. Perhaps like me, you went from cop to cakes!

If you don't manage to get the press involved just yet, never give up. There are lots of PR (public relation companies) out there who give free advice on how to get free publicity.

I personally am a fan of Jo Swann, from Chocolate PR who uses her Facebook group to give out lots of free advice about how to get the media interested in your business. Take a look as she has some great ideas.

Jo, and Chocolate PR can be found at www.chocolatepr.co.uk

If you can't get any media attention for your cake business launch/relaunch then ask a friend, who is very good at taking photographs, to pop down and take lots of pictures for your social media.

Now I'm not a control freak, but I would direct which shots you want taken of the launch and check how your friend is getting on. I have made the mistake of asking a family member to take photographs of me at a similar event, where I had my cakes business on display, and ended up with great pictures of the venues bins and toilets together with my cakes. Not what I wanted and no amount of photo cropping afterward helped either.

By the way, you don't have to have one big bang cake business launch. You could do lots of mini-events in the same week. The idea of this cake business launch will help you focus on getting stuff done, rather than just thinking it.

I regularly advise on launches/relaunches with the cake business clients that I coach, my 'Cakepreneurs'. We set a date during our bi-weekly or monthly coaching sessions, where we set their launch or relaunch date and their activities in the run-up to it. I promise you that it really does get them working on their list of things to do and makes them accountable to me!

So plan launch day or launch week for your cake business.

Here is another suggestion for the launch/relaunch of your cake business.

Host a launch party at home, or at a relative's home, if yours is too small. Host it together with friends and other local influencers from your networking circles.

By networking circles I mean people you meet at the gym, the nursery, library, hairdressers or women's club. You don't have to be a member or attendee of a networking group to network.

An 'influencer' is someone who is your ideal cake customer, or who has friends and family (especially on Facebook) who are your ideal cake customer. They have fingers in many pies and could help ideal customers to find out as they network in the right circles.

You may need to attract these 'influencers' to your event by giving away cakes or maybe you know a beautician or hairdresser, who would like to join you and offer a free session or prize draw at the event.

Make it an evening or weekend event with cake and fizz (Aldi does some very nice fizz for 4 pounds), (Come on now, I'm not a cheapskate, it's just I'm keeping an eye on your marketing budget here.).

At the event get your guests to check in on Facebook at the event, and tweet or post on Instagram about it. (You will need to set an event up on Facebook for guests to check into, if you haven't got a location in your business name set up at the location you host your cake business launch at.)

Don't forget every contact counts. Make it a charity event and also invite the local press. Plan this right and it will be an inexpensive marketing success.

Combine this event with others that week and ensure that your ideal cake customer is at the forefront of your mind at all times.

We are going for gold with your cake business, so be careful not to attract the wrong type of cake customer, the cheap cake hunter!

Of course you don't have to relaunch if you are confident that your cake brand is strong enough already and you are happy with it the way it is.

You could just have a new range of cakes to launch, as you refresh your cake range, or simply add a new showstopper cake to your portfolio. Any excuse really.

Chapter 7: Marketing Online - Social Media, Web Sites and Blogs

What is Online Marketing

Let's face it, it's the 21st-century, and you can't ignore it social media and web sites are here to stay.

These online platforms are your cake shop window at the very least! They are a representation of your cake business brand, your online brochure, and a marketing tool, but most importantly they show your ideal cake customer, who you are, in the way you speak, your text and copy, your values and your business values!

I can't stress enough here that you must use at least one social media platform, as well as your web site, if not instead of your website.

Online marketing is huge and it doesn't have to cost a lot or anything at all in fact.

In chapter 3, we discussed identifying your ideal cake customers, and hopefully by now you have a detailed outline of your ideal cake customer groups up on a wall somewhere, or even stuck to your fridge, together with your goals, vision and your mission statement.

I would be over the moon if you had given your groups names and faces too!

Being home based is difficult, but it's not impossible to succeed in the cake business, believe me, as most successful cake business owners started from home.

(Jo Malone, the candle, scents and cologne company was started by a woman in her home. I know it's not a cake business, but she filled her tiny home with all the ingredients and bottles she needed, so comparable to a cake making business).

If you had a cake store, you would meet and see the faces of your ideal cake customers physically in there. You would know their names and maybe a bit about them as you pass the time of day serving them.

But, being home based means you can only imagine them, most of the time, and that's where your avatar groups really help you.

With a home based cake business, you need to look to social media, and or a web site, as your shop or store. It can be more than just your shop window on the outside with your excellent branding and pictures. Your social media can also replicate the inside of your cake shop, a place where you can chat and get to know more about your customers, and more importantly they can get to know you, your values and everything else that makes your cake business special.

A website isn't a must in my mind initially as much as social media platforms are, but if you can, I would have both. A website can mean a large investment initially, if you want one with all

the whistles and bells on, which may have to come out of your marketing budget, or you can pop the cost onto your operating costs in year one, so therefore needs careful planning and consideration.

We will discuss web sites later in this chapter, but for now let's concentrate on social media online marketing.

Social media marketing should not be looked at in isolation, you should always have a good mix of online and offline marketing.

Social media marketing isn't all about paid adverts either.

Your cake business social media marketing can actually be all 'organic' and free by getting people to share your posts and engage with you.

By organic I mean a post that gets liked and shared because of its contents. It could be a vegan or gluten free cupcake recipe you have developed or found. Both these niches are big and growing on the internet as we speak

Facebook defines it as "the total number of unique people shown you post through unpaid distribution".

My first rule of thumb is that exhaust free organic marketing first before you spend a penny on paid adverts.

It is safe to assume that most of your 'avatars', your ideal cake customers are on at least one social media platform. But don't guess this, find out!

When considering which method of marketing online or offline is most cost effective, as far as your marketing budget and your time is concerned a very simple evaluation will help you.

Now don't get concerned, an evaluation can be as simple as a piece of paper with five vertical columns on it.

In the first column, on the left hand side, write down the marketing activity you undertook, or are thinking of undertaking. Both online and offline.

Such as a networking day/evening, a wedding fair, a school fete or an advert on a social media platform, such as Instagram, Facebook or Twitter.

On the remaining four columns, along the top, put a heading of 'Cost of Event/Advert', Number of Leads', 'Number of Sales' and 'Time Taken'.

Cost of the event/ advert includes travel cost, if any.

Number of leads means email addresses/telephone numbers/new social media followers. But remember only those that you consider to be your ideal cake customer count. Don't cheat as you're cheating yourself here.

Number of sales, this may be orders taken as a result of that activity, or deposits taken.

Time taken is important, as time is money.

In our working example earlier we put aside 20 hours a week for cake business admin and marketing. Posting on social media or attending an event is time taken out of this 20 hours and therefore you will need to make sure you use your time effectively.

It might surprise you when you add up the amount of time taken in preparing for a wedding fair with the travel time and time at the show!

For a Facebook advert you may have to learn and use a system to create wonderful graphics for a post. This will also eat into your admin time.

So let's expand on this.

For example:

£50 to have a table at a wedding fair with cake samples and leaflets £10. 10 hours for the event including preparation and travel time.

Compared to:

£60 spent on Facebook and/or Instagram adverts, 4 hours designing and placing adverts on social media.

How many leads or orders did you get from either form of marketing?

Don't jump to any conclusions until all the columns are filled in, but you can see the way it is going.

It's not exactly a scientific evaluation, but I suggest you compare a few events and see what works best for you, your business, your family/work life balance, and working towards your goal of running a successful cake business.

So you can start to see the advantages of social media marketing straight away, in this crude two dimensional example.

Whether you are already using social media or are about to start there are certain things that you need to know.

Firstly I will state the obvious, well obvious to some. Social media accounts are free. It's only paid adverts that spend your marketing budget.

There is of course the time it takes to manage your social media account or accounts, and whilst you are doing this you aren't making cakes or developing new products so there is a cost in time.

You may not be up to date with the ever changing 'algorithm changes' affecting each social media platform, and therefore this time away from your cakes and your family might be a bridge too far, as the rules seem to change by the minute these days.

Just a reminder here from chapter 1. To be successful in the cake business we must ensure that we learn at all times. Well I think keeping up with what's happening with social media trends and algorithms is one such learning activity you can't afford to miss out on.

Just find a really good Facebook group which keeps you updated in a simple and effective way is my advice. .

I also highly recommend getting a social media 'expert 'to manage your social media accounts for you as soon as you can.

What I mean by expert, is someone who knows what they are doing.

This could be a family member, or you could outsource it to a paid social media manager. There are plenty about and you can choose how much you want to spend out of your marketing budget on outsourcing.

One of my favourite social media managers is on Facebook and Instagram is Kimberley Banner.

She listens and gets on board with brands so quickly and is full of great ideas. I feel that she is totally part of the team and her web site blogs are so helpful. Again more free advice from the experts.

Find free social media advice at www.kimberleybanner.com

Or maybe look at other social media accounts you like and ask who manages them.

I would definitely recommend as your cake business grows, you build in the cost of outsourcing your social media management, to allow you to do what you do best and concentrate on your cakes .Maybe not now, but it is worth considering it in the future.

But, and it's a big but! It's your cake brand, in its colours, vibe, and values. It is your personality and voice that you want coming through via your social media posts.

Your posts are the biggest representation of your cake brand that your ideal customers will see, so don't allow this to be weakened or go off brand.

You must direct what you want it to look, feel and sound like. You are the boss, so find a social media manager/friend that you can work with, and who listens to you.

Take advice by all means, and maybe rebrand if you need to with a new logo and/or colours etc., but never give full control to someone else. Let them do the work in consultation with you or under your direction. It is your cake business, your goal and your vision.

I fell foul of this in the early days of social media, allowing a friends younger family member to do what teenagers do best, use social media. How wrong was I? So choose wisely if you do pass the running of your cake business social media accounts on.

So, what social media platforms are out there?

Facebook, Instagram, Pinterest, Twitter, and LinkedIn. By the time you read this book there are possibly some new kids on the block, but I will concentrate on these.

So now you need to understand a little bit more about these social media platforms and what they can and can't do as a representation of your cake shop and marketing tool.

You can split the platforms up into two groups.

Business to Business Marketing (B2B)

Marketing to other businesses and organisations. They may want to buy their customers or employees cakes as a gift. The 'Get Well Soon' cupcakes to employees are always popular, as well as large cupcake orders for a show or corporate event, like a car launch or gallery opening.

Business to Customer Marketing (B2C)

This is marketing directly to your customer base with wedding, engagement, and birthday cakes etc.

All social media platforms are good for both groups you could say, but it essential that you know your audience when using social media, and that you listen to what they want, and pick your social media channel accordingly.

If your cake business success is via large corporate orders, then you may want to concentrate on B2B social media marketing.

I personally recommend using Twitter and LinkedIn for B2B marketing. For B2C I would suggest Facebook and Instagram, and then Pinterest.

But please remember, you may have the best social media posts ever seen, and may spend a fortune, in time and money, on making them, but if the social media post for your cake business are sat on the wrong platform, no one will read them and you will have wasted your time and possibly money.

With social media you can also connect with other local businesses in your area. These other businesses may not be your ideal cake customers, but they may be potential suppliers or business collaborators, or other businesses which complement yours like florists, wedding outfitters and photographers for example.

By using your business social media accounts, you can like or comment on these other businesses posts as a way of forging alliances into working together. If you are seen commenting and interacting with them, their customers may follow and like your cake business too!

Don't forget to:

• Comment and like as your cake business though, and not as you personally.

- Don't forget to be current as there is nothing worse than old news. Try and bring about discussions on cakey topics on your social media.

- Post regularly in your cake businesses social media accounts, but don't blitz it for a few weeks, and then leave it .Old posts speak volumes.

- Don't forget to actually market your social media platforms too. A strange concept, but what I mean is tell people you are on Facebook, Instagram or Twitter etc. Make sure you have all your social media addresses on all your communications. From your email signature, to leaflets, business cards and posters.

It is not a case of 'build it and they will come ', you need to let potential cake customers know you are on social media and your social media addresses.

But, before I go into the five most common social media platforms, I must just remind you to have fun!

Your customers are people and no one is serious all the time. Make sure you make them smile occasionally or even all the time. People buy people, so be human.

Cake Business to Business Marketing

Now I have listed the main social media platforms to interact directly with your ideal cake customers, let's take a look at the ones I would personally use for B2B.Twitter and LinkedIn.

Twitter

I love twitter and especially as a networking tool and for selling to other businesses.

In its basic form, a twitter post is just to show you are a cake business in a particular area, and to showcase your cakes.

At its next level, your twitter post can drive traffic to your website blog. The increased traffic to your website, in theory, means you may climb higher up any search engines, like Google, and be found more easily. This can be achieved by writing a blog, posting it on your website and when people see your post highlighting the blog and they find it interesting, they may click on a link which takes them to website.

Right here is the scary bit, the more you tweet quality posts, with quality pictures, the more engagement you will have. I have been asked what is the right number of times to tweet a day and the answer would blow you away. As many times as you can, I always reply.

You can take a blog from your website (if you have one), and this blog can be broken down into a number of clever tweets used with different titles at different times.

Once you get the hang of it, you can look at the times of day your ideal customers, potential collaborators, or even influencers are online and target those times with scheduled tweets. There are quite a few tweet scheduling platforms which I have used over time.

Look out for the hashtag (#hours) in your chosen cake selling area on twitter.

Hashtag hours are great for networking with businesses. I live in Birmingham, England, and the first hashtag hour I found was #Brumhour, which I joined in with every Sunday night at 8pm by just putting #Brumhour in the search bar and following.

I met loads of local businesses and learnt about them and they learnt about me and my cake business.

Every time I posted on twitter and included @Brumhour, they have retweeted my tweet to their 22K followers, for Free!

There are lots of #hours during the day, if you get a bit lonely in your cake kitchen. Most will retweet for free too.

There's plenty of baking and cake related hashtag hours too.

LinkedIn

LinkedIn has more of the look of Facebook look to it these days, and is the platform where historically professionals looked for professional career/networking opportunities.

But if you have left a career, or job behind, to focus on your cake business success, then you will most likely already have a profile and lots of ex co-workers, who may have tasted your fantastic cakes already .

Therefore don't turn your back on these potential ideal cake customers. You have already built a relationship with them in another profession, just change your skill base on LinkedIn and promote yourself as the professional cake business owner that you are now.

Just update your profile and ensure it is kept up to date. Again nothing speak louder than an out of date profile

Short and sweet buts that's my take on LinkedIn.

Let's discuss hashtags in a bit more detail. They are used for customers to find cake businesses in their area, or specific types of cake such as eggless or vegan.

There are many uses of the hashtag so make sure you use them, whether it is on Twitter, Facebook, Instagram or Pinterest.

Hashtag your USP and your preferred ideal cake customer location at every chance you get.

With Instagram the unwritten hashtag rule is about 30 hashtags after your post, but with other platforms it is less. Keep a scratch pad on your phone or laptop of your hashtags and maybe look at the analytics for their popularity.

For example, I have just looked on Instagram at ' #weddingcake' and there were 3 million posts to choose from. Put an 'S' on the end and ' #weddingcakes' goes down to 490,000 posts.

You want to choose a lower number of hashtag impressions so that your post will be seen in your chosen cake selling area, but no so low that no one will find it.

So be more specific with, for example #vintageweddingcake was even lower today with 3,868 posts.

Going for a location with #weddingcakesbirmingham gave me 640 posts to look at on Instagram.

One way of measuring the success of a hashtag is to post almost identical content, but vary the hashtag, and see what the difference is in the interaction.

At the end of the day you want your cake business to be found and not swamped and lost in a sea of other posts.

Before I go any further though I must mention the 80/20 rule! This rule applies to all social media platforms but I thought it best to mention it now.

I compare this rule to a good Victoria sponge cake. 80 % cake, 20 % buttercream. I love buttercream me.

The 'cake' is general posts of interest, ideas, recipes, funny cake or wedding related facts etc., it's not directly selling your cakes or services or your cake business. It is not self-promoting. It just helps address your ideal customer's pain points, or maybe their baking issues and shows them who you are, your personality, and your brand.

The 'buttercream' is the self-promoting posts. Directly telling your ideal cake customer about your cakes and products.

No one wants to see post, after post, after post of direct marketing from you, as they will switch off, and unfollow you. They want to see your personality, learn stuff and be entertained. So with all your social media posts keep to the 80/20 rule.

Cake Business to Your Ideal Customer Marketing

So next let's look at online social media marketing to get your fabulous cake business out there and seen by your ideal cake customers, who want celebration and wedding cakes .This is B2C cake businesses marketing.

The best platforms for this I find are Facebook, Instagram and Pinterest.

(Don't forget these sites are free, it is only when you decide, and if you decide, to spend money on expanding your circulation that you pay for an advert)

Facebook

Most of you will have heard of Facebook and use it regularly. This is the all-rounder increasingly being used, more and more by every generation.

In its simplest form a Facebook business page has many uses for your cake business.

Having a Facebook business page in the cake business is a MUST for me. I would suggest that you set up your business Facebook page at the same time, or even before your web site.

It is an online representation of your cake business and it can also serve as your online brochure and it can be used as a marketing tool.

As I mentioned before, it is a fabulous medium to use to actually talk to your ideal cake customers and address their frustrations and issues by posting helpful hints, tips and videos, so that they can build a relationship with you.

Most cake business owners forget to do this, and use their social media sites just to pump out more and more self-promotion of their cake business. Stick to the 80/20 rule!

At a more advanced level, Facebook can be used to sell your cakes, cake related goods and equipment, and add to your income streams for your cake business whilst still adhering to the 80/20 rule.

Even if you haven't the time to dive in and use Facebook as an active marketing tool, just ensure it is kept up to date, as it will serve as a simple brochure showcasing your work.

If you simply want to use it as your shop window / brochure, I suggest that your logo goes into the profile picture, and a montage of your cakes, or a picture of yourself next to your showstopper cake (head and shoulders) serves as your cover picture, Don't forget people buy people, so smile.

Ensure that your cakes are photographed well, and on brand!

Once again a Facebook business page is FREE, but it must be linked to your Facebook personal profile account. Your cake business Facebook page cannot have 'friends' like a personal page, but will collect likes and therefore followers.

Facebook will take down any business page that sets up as a personal page.

Let's make it clear to you straight from the start, Facebook is a business. It exists to make money and will prioritise those posts that are paid for adverts. This makes using Facebook as a marketing channel more and more complex, but don't let that deter you.

You possibly wonder why you don't see posts from a particular person or group that you are following anymore on Facebook in your news feed.

Well it's simple. Facebook cannot send you every post from every person/group that you follow or are interested in. It does a little bit of science in the background (called an algorithm) and looks to see which person/ group you have interacted with recently.(By interact I mean like or comment on their posts) .

So it is vital that you get your followers to interact with you regularly by asking questions and getting them to like and comment on posts.

Facebook is changing rapidly, and it would be a little bit of a waste of time to go into too much detail about the current intricacy of Facebook in 2018, as it will have changed as soon as this book goes to print.

That said, it is important that your brand identity on Facebook is up to date, and at the very least shows you and your cakes. You can put links to your website, and display your contact number, and even manage your ideal cake customers' expectations of how you wish to be contacted, and how long it will take for you to reply via a pinned post.

Don't forget on your own personal page to state that you are owner of 'The Cake Business 'and cross reference to events happening on your cake business page .

My advice is if you can learn just one social media platform, and do it well, Facebook is the one.

Instagram

It is said that there is more engagement on Instagram than on Facebook! The jury is out as far as I'm concerned, but make sure your ideal customer uses Instagram before you commit valuable marketing time to this platform.

Instagram has a dreaded algorithm, like Facebook, and relies on likes and comments to judge your popularity, so keep your followers engaged and they might actually get to see your posts.

The key is to keep your followers engaged and commenting. Turn on your notifications so that you can be notified when someone wants to engage with you, as this may be a potential ideal cake customer.

Make sure you choose a business Instagram account, as it is much better than a normal one. An Instagram business page links to your Facebook business page, and it has analytics too, If you want to see how well or which type of posts perform best. You can also add your contact details to a business page so customers can contact you directly from Instagram.

It only allows one link in your profile so consider using a Link tree link which can expand showing all your other links too. Useful for links to your blogs. If you don't know what I mean take a look at my Instagram profile @cakebizcoach

Instagram also allows you to post a location. Great to show customers where you are if you're setting up a wedding cake at a swanky hotel somewhere. This might be seen by other couples researching the venue for their wedding.

Instagram is very visually based, so your pictures need to be high quality. Low quality pictures and settings can damage your cake business on Instagram.

Instagram has now released an Instagram stories function, which allows you to add posts that only stay on your feed for 24hrs.

The nice thing about the Instagram stories function, for your cake business, is it allows you to be you for 24 hours, maybe showing a behind the scenes photo or video allowing your followers to see the person behind the cake business is actually human. These stories don't have to be as polished may be as the normal Instagram posts that stay up for ever on your site .

The downside of Instagram, for me, is that scheduling your posts is more difficult, as it appears that when posting using a desktop computer or a laptop, there is less functionality than when using Instagram on your tablet or phone. Hopefully this has also been resolved by the time the book is published.

You can use a scheduler like Hootsuite on the laptop, but I prefer to use my phone to post. Therefore the downside to Instagram for me is that you need to be present, posting, tagging and liking.

Pinterest

Pinterest a highly underutilised social media platform. Firstly it isn't really a social media platform. Pinterest is really a search engine, and place to connect with your ideal cake customer and to sell your cakes and services.

Pinterest is a link back to your cake business website in its basic function. You need to consider what problems you can solve for your ideal cake customer when you are posting stuff on Pinterest.

Consider posting a picture and a link to an article you have written on how to plan a child's cupcake decorating birthday party perhaps, and the picture links back to a blog you wrote on your website.

Again this increases traffic to your web site and helps it climb the rankings when customers search for cake makers 'in my area 'on Google.

Try and think how can I be helpful?

If it's mainly the celebration cake that you are concentrating you could develop Pinterest posts that help your followers/customer with the planning of a birthday party, birthday party theme ideas. How to make a unicorn party game or how to decorate your child's party in a unicorn theme.

If it is the wedding cake market you are focusing on then posts relating to weddings, engagements, wedding speeches etc. This is a simplification, but hopefully it will help you understand how it works.

Like Facebook it does have a sort of algorithm a "smart feed". It looks at what you are interested in, and keywords.

Pinterest is a search engine so think of it in that way.

In relation to all the social media platforms, as well as having my cake business calendar planner, I also had a social media marketing planner.

This is a calendar with important and relevant dates on, so that I could plan my posts on Facebook, Instagram and Twitter well in advance. It also allowed me to follow the 80/20 rule.

A sample of this year's social media calendar included the royal wedding, International women's day, St George's day etc.

I would start planning my posts and promotion for Valentines and Mother's Day some six weeks ahead on social media, and similarly with my Christmas cake marketing campaigns.

Always sticking to the 80/20 rule so that I was careful I didn't switch my followers off. This enabled me to find the time to write helpful blogs on making the perfect mince pies or vegan Christmas cakes ready for my campaigns.

Websites, Blogs, and Photographing Your Cakes

If you really want to make your cake business a success, although not essential in the start-up phase, then you will need a website.

A website in its simplest form is your shop window or it could in fact be your cake shop.

I am almost certain that your ideal cake customer uses a search engine such as Google to locate their cake makers etc. It is the 21st century.

Even my 83 yr. old mother gets out her tablet and Googles 'gardeners in my area' to find local services. It is a fact that most of us use our mobile phones or tablets to locate products or services on a daily basis and that goes for finding cake suppliers like yourself.

Why is this seemly random fact important to you as a cake business owner? Well when I go on to talk about websites below you will be amazed at the number of websites out there, both cake makers and other types, who have not considered or designed their web sites to be viewed on a mobile phone! I find it off putting when I can't see all of the site.

I think that nearly everyone uses their mobile phones now to search on Google, well in the UK they do.

If you have or are going to have a cake business website, make sure you test out what it looks like on a mobile whilst building it or having it built .

Seriously, you will be amazed how different it looks. You don't want the top of your showstopper cake to be cut off when viewed on a mobile phone after all.

So cake business websites. For me there are two sorts of web site .A brochure site, which as the name says is an online brochure for your cake business, and an e commerce site.

A brochure website in its simplest form is your cake shop window. This is important if you are a home based cake business, or even if you are shop based, and have a great window display, this is your second shop window.

There are build it yourself brochure websites with the likes of 'Go Daddy' and ' Wix' which are very easy to build and cheap to run. It can be just one page to begin with, but at least your cake business has an online presence.

You may want to take your website to the next level and have a two page 'brochure' site. By two pages I mean one can be your homepage to display a sample of your work, and the other page could be your 'blog' to bring social media traffic to your website. This will in turn should pull your website up the Google rankings. I will discuss blogging separately.

Then there is an ecommerce website. This is a website where you can actually take payments online for your cakes, products or services.

It is another way of monetising your website, as it can provide other income streams if you want to start selling other cake related products by having a shop on your website.

Finally in this website section is blogging .You can have a blog page on your web site as the second page or you can simply have just a blog page full stop.

It will not be a shop window for your beautiful cakes though, but it will say more about you as a professional cake business owner and it can be another income generator with the use of things such as google AdWords to name but a few things that you can do to monetise your blogs.

Vlogs are also becoming more popular.

If you are just starting out on your journey to cake business success, as I have said before, it is not essential to have a website, as your Facebook and Instagram sites can work extremely well as your shop window, but a website can help in providing other income streams more effectively than a social media platform.

You may have decided now is the time for the 'Full Monty' of web sites and you want to outsource the building of it to a professional.

I strongly recommend you get lots of quotes from web designers, but don't be talked into something you can't afford at the start, keep in budget and add pages at a later stage as your cake business develops.

Here is some more advice regarding outsourcing the development of your cake business website, given from my own experiences.

1. Ensure it is mobile friendly as 80% of websites are viewed via mobile devices.
2. Be on 'Brand' with the design and content. It's your cake business.
3. Ensure that you buy the domain name, and it's registered to you.
4. The website needs to be 'hung' on the internet and hosted. Make sure you discuss where the web site will be hosted, and that you pay for the yearly hosting fee. Your cake business website is a very valuable asset and giving others control or ownership of it is fraught with issues.
5. Your website will need updating, with you constantly adding new blogs and pictures. Make sure that you have access to the back end of the web site and the basic knowledge to do these things, or talk to the web developer about managing this for you. Ask for the price per item uploaded, and the service level agreement of how long it will take the web developer to action your changes to your website.

If all of the above has made you think, oh no! Why not invest in doing a simple website course, and build your own website.

Lots of cake business owners are doing this now and believe me it's far simpler these days as the web site packages have built in 'idiot' guides to help people like me.

Photographing your cakes.

As you have seen from the social media marketing sections previously, it is crucial for the success of your cake business to have great quality photographs.

Great quality in terms of composition, lighting, on brand and of course picture quality. One good cake picture goes a long way and so does a bad one!
Take your time with photographing your cakes as good cake photographs are your best asset.

I have said many times that especially with your wedding cakes, it is worth investing in professional pictures being taken. Make sure you direct the photographer as to your brand identity, the staging and style, it's your photoshoot.

Consider teaming up with a wedding photographer and do some cross business promotion. Maybe even get down to a cost neutral arrangement in exchange for promoting their pictures on your social media.

I am always watching the marketing budget you see.

But, if you are keen to take your own photographs of your delicious creations, here are a few tips to help you along.

1. Use natural light. Photograph them outside, perhaps on the garden table, even on a grey damp morning.
2. If you haven't purchased a cake backdrop, then use a white background so that it doesn't compete with the detail and the colours on your cake.
3. Maybe add staging and props to the picture such as flowers or lace gloves or a string of beads which go down well with vintage cupcakes particularly.
4. Most mobile phones have fabulous cameras on them these days, so don't be afraid to play with the settings and angles of your pictures. You don't need a super expensive camera.
5. Take lots of different pictures and isolate the detail on your cakes in a few of your shots.
6. Maybe invest in one of those photographic tents if taking pictures outside is not an option.

Finally, just a few words about email marketing.

We have discussed collecting email contact details as leads for potential ideal cake customers via a 'Goldfish Bowl' competition. These emails can be used to inform potential cake customers of your new cake range or another new cake service that you are offering.

I suggest if you are going to use a free email marketing platform you look at 'Mailchimp' as a way to create your engaging mailshots to your potential cake customers.

Mailchimp is a widely used trusted platform enabling you to email up to 2000 email addresses a day with your cake campaigns for free.

Chapter 8: The Legal Stuff

Food Hygiene, Cleaning Regimes, Allergens and Flowers on Cakes

There is so much that I have learned over the years in the cake business that I was beginning to think that I needed a degree in law, especially contract law, to protect my cake business and myself. Luckily I had already studied contract law many moons ago, and had a basic understanding.

Don't worry, you won't have to study law as there is plenty of help and advice out there including what I am going to tell you in this chapter, so sit back and relax.

My basic advice is tell it as it is. I believe honesty is key.

If you have frozen your cakes, because you freeze after batch baking, then tell the customer if they ask.

Also suggest to them that they pop into the local supermarket, and ask how many of their cakes were frozen before they reached the display aisle!

It is a nightmare baking on demand, so don't be ashamed if you do batch bake and then freeze. This is a business.

If the customer demands a freshly baked cake then they must understand that due to time scales this will lessen the decorating time, and more staff may be required to assist in creating their perfect cake, and the price may reflect this. It might actually be part of your USP to bake on demand and therefore let everyone know this.

Food Hygiene Regulations

There are lots of elements to the Food Hygiene Regulations 2006, but if you have taken a 'Level 2 Food Safety and Hygiene' course and you have downloaded, or obtained a copy of 'Safer Food, Better Business' pack you will know enough to start your cake business.

I personally recommend the Virtual College Level 2 Food Safety online course. It took me about 3 hours, over a couple of days, to complete but it wasn't difficult. It is a pass or fail course though.

There is no legal requirement to hold this qualification, and no legal requirement to renew it every three years, but most Environmental Health Departments (EHD) expect that you have studied it.

The Safer Food, Better Business pack you can actually get from your local EHD, or you can download it from their website. I would try asking for a copy though at first as it drains your printer inks.

I must admit that there is a great deal in the pack, and indeed the Level 2 online course, that does not relate to running a cake businesses, but they are both a must in my mind. Your local EHD may insist that you fill out your 'Safer Food, Better Business' pack before they make their inspection.

I spoke to a lady the other day who said that her EHD don't even come out to inspect her business, they just send out a questionnaire every so often!

The number one alignment that concerns the Environmental Health Officers (EHOs) that come out to inspect me is a poorly tummy. Fortunately I have a cast iron stomach and I rarely suffer, but the rule with a poorly tummy is, stay away from cakes!

You should wait at least 48 hours after an upset tum has stopped, before you start making cakes again.

I am not an EHO, or a doctor, so whatever the alignment that has decided to take hold of you, and or your household members, go and get advice regarding handling food and making cakes from your doctor, EHO or the EHD website.

Don't forget after the period of illness has passed you will need to do an extra deep clean of your kitchen, using your approved cleaning materials with antibacterial wipes of all handles, doors and cupboards.

Again I am not an EHO so always seek advice.

By law in the UK you must register with your local authority EHD in order to run a cake business.

They may come out and inspect your kitchen or your premises. Give them a call or look online for their local procedures on how to register. It does differ greatly across the whole of the UK from one local authority to another.

They usually say that if you haven't been inspected within 28 days of registering, then you can start selling your cakes after the 28 days. But, as I say, please check with your local authority first on this as it may change.

The EHO comes to visit

Once you have registered with the local authority as I said you may be inspected.

If you are inspected, it may not be an EHO who comes out, but another person representing the local authority and the Foods Standards Agency. Whomever it is, it is always a pleasure to see them, and I could write another book on my many varied visits. There is only one thing to understand though, they are there to help you.

Here are a few things that you can do in readiness for their visit.

1. Have your Safer Food, Better Business to hand and filled in.
2. Have your Level 2 Food Hygiene Certificate ready.
3. Have your cleaning schedule typed up and a full list of the products you use when cleaning.
4. Make sure your first aid box has blue plasters in .
5. Make sure you have a separate fridge thermometer, independent of what the fridge is registering.
6. Have your public liability Insurance to hand

The list goes on, and each local authority has its own set of rules, so try and find out what they are before your register.

Rules regarding washing machines in the same room as you are making your cakes, and where your hand washing sink is located, also varies across the authorities, but be mindful of these two possible issues.

As I say, they, the EHD are there to help you, so don't dread the visit.

Following your inspection you will be awarded a Food Standards Agency rating.

Food labelling in the cake business

Please read and refer to the Foods Standards Agency Website for up to date information on the latest list of allergens, and the rules relating to them in your cake business.

At the time of writing this book there are 14 major allergens listed, which must be mentioned in the ingredients of any food products sold and this includes your cakes.

Even if you weren't selling your cake and you were giving cake away, say for charity, I would still list the cake ingredients and especially the allergens.

The main allergens are:

Allergens containing gluten
,crustaceans,eggs,fish,peanuts,nuts,celery,mustard,soybeans,milk ,molluscs,sesame seeds, Sulphur dioxide and Sulphites Lupin .

Now I personally list all my cake ingredients and put a sticker on the cake box, or a printed list inside with all of my cakes.

Also on my cake quote I clearly ask that I be informed immediately of any allergies that could affect the making of the cake. The most common one I have found is a nut allergy, especially when you are thinking of using a chocolate replacement spread, like Nutella. It has caught a few of my fellow cake makers out before. Always check the ingredients with whatever you are using.

Bottom line is I ask to be informed when I am filling out the cake order form/contract of any dietary requirements or allergies and I ask again on the cake quote if one is given.

Flowers on cakes

Fresh flowers on cakes are another minefield, and I personally dissuaded my cake customers from having real flowers on their cakes, as they can cause issues in relation to insects etc. This is apart from the fact that the flowers the customer usually chooses are the poisonous ones!

Fresh flowers also tend to wilt quickly too, and make the cake look quite awful after it has been sat in a warm room for a while.

There are some fabulous silk flowers about which look exactly like the real ones, if you haven't got the skills or the time to replicate the flowers in florist paste.

But that is my take on real flowers on cakes and things to be considered. It is your cake business.

I have spoken to a few cake makers who say as long as you protect the stems of the flowers, when they are inserted into the cake, you are okay. I am not convinced myself.

If you are tempted to use real flowers, first ensure they are not poisonous and they MUST be organic. Pesticide free flowers.

A good rule of thumb is when in doubt leave it out if you are uncertain as to whether they are organic flowers. But if you do flowers on your cake then a barrier must always be used between the flower and the cake, and the flowers are not allowed to touch the cake.

I would also put a sign up, and include on my ingredient list, that the flowers are not edible and should not be consumed.

The nightmare gets worse when a bride or groom has instructed a florist to decorate the cake or supply the flowers at the venue.

I would suggest that you liaise with the florist beforehand and ensure that he or she adheres to the food safety precautions in relations to the flowers. If this is not possible I would get a disclaimer signed by the customer that you supplied the cake only and take no responsibility for the flowers used to decorate it.

There are of course edible flowers which can be used on cakes. Again I would use extreme caution even with edible flowers, as consuming them in large quantities is not recommended, and not all of the flower may be edible, it may only be the petals!

It's your reputation, your livelihood at stake here, so tread carefully with flowers on cakes please.

Tax, Local Council, Insurances and Landlords

As a sole trader you are taxed as an individual, and as the owner of a limited company your company has to pay corporation tax and you still have to pay tax on your wages.

In both scenarios you are also liable for national insurance.

You need to inform HMRC that you are the owner of a new business and register with them even if you are already paying tax and national insurance in another job.

The one issue for me is, that most cake business owners start their cake businesses whilst working in another career or job.

At the time of going to print your tax free personal allowance is £11,850. If you have another role your tax free allowance may possibly be linked to that role.

Therefore when you pay tax on your second income, your cake business wage, you will have to pay tax on everything you earn, as your tax free allowance may not be available.

This is where a taking the advice of an accountant is key to ensure you allow for this.

The higher rate of tax is also payable at 40 % on earnings over £46,351. So if your first income and your cake business income is liable to take you into the higher rate of tax bracket. I would definitely seek professional advice as there may a more cost effective way of paying your tax if you are a limited company.

I am not an accountant, and I do not seek to give your financial tax advice. All I can ask is that you do seek out a friendly and helpful accountant to guide you in these matters.

Insurances

There are many types of insurances that you need to consider when running a cake business.

Firstly if you are using your own vehicle for your cake business, going to consultations, shopping for the business, or delivering cakes then you will need business vehicle insurance even if it is your family car 90% of the time.

That is not a big issue, I hear many people say, but if you don't cover your vehicle with business insurance just imagine the following scenario.

Through no fault of your own you have a collision in your car, whilst delivering a cake, or whilst you have a bulky cake ingredient shop in the boot.

The Police attend the scene of your accident and they ask you about the cake, or the boot full of flour and eggs, and what you were doing at the time of the accident.

You tell them that you were delivering a cake as part of your business, or you were shopping for your cake business! The truth is always best.

The Police then check the vehicle database and see that you do not have business insurance for your vehicle. You are then using your vehicle without insurance and they have the right to seize your vehicle, with the cake on board and you will be left stranded and looking at a big fine and points on your license.

I know that this is an extreme example but it is correct and imagine the impact this would have not only on your day, but your cake business!

Public liability insurance is also a must for your cake business, as it protects anyone who is made unwell, or was injured as a result of your cake business. You will find that to have a stall at most events, including a wedding fare the organisers may ask to see your public liability insurance certificate first.

The EHO may ask to inspect it when they come out to visit you too.

When you expand your cake business and employ someone else to assist you, by law you will need employer's liability insurance too.

If you are running a cake business from home you will need to speak to your household insurance company, as they may not cover certain household items like your oven fridge and mixer, and therefore you will need to consider taking out a separate insurance.

So having registered with the local council, you now need to find out if you are liable for business rates, even if you are operating your cake business from home. You may have to pay business rates on the part of your property that you use for your cake business.

To check if you need to pay business rates contact the Valuation Office Agency, the VOA, and explain to them the part of your premises you use for your business.

You can find the VOA at www.gov.uk.

Make sure that you tell them if the area you use for your cake business is multi-functional as a home as well as a business, and what proportion of time that area of your home is used as a business.

Another consideration is operating your cake business from a rented property. You will need to inform your landlord and get their permission. The same can be said for your mortgage provider. Some providers have clauses prohibiting you from operating a business from the mortgaged property.

One of my 'Cakepreneurs' contacted me after she had informed her landlord that she had started a cake business. The landlord informed her that she was not permitted to do this as it would mean him applying for a change of use for her flat. I personally looked into this for her and advised him that in fact a change of use was not required.

Again I am not a legal expert and I strongly advise you always take legal advice when situations like this occur.

Cake Contracts, Deposits

As I mentioned previously, I feel as though you need to be a barrister sometimes when you are running a cake business, to mitigate against all those little issues that could arise when supplying cakes.

But fear not, most of the issues can be covered with cake contracts, disclaimers and clear policies.

You can also use the term cake order form, but I personally like referring to them as cake order contracts because that is what they are. I feel it focuses me and the cake customer on the fact that this is a legal contract if filled out correctly.

For me there are three types of cake contract that you need for your cake business, together with a clear and concise refund and deposit policy, which I would have on your cake business website if possible.

The three contracts are

- cake order contract/form
- wedding cake order contract/form
- cake hand over form.

I personally keep my cake and wedding cake contracts separate, as I do tend to put more detail on the wedding cake contract, but it is entirely up to you to decide if you want to use one cake order form for both.

I have placed a downloadable version of each of these forms on my website to help you, so pop along and take a look. You will find them at :

www.thecakebizcoach.com

Please feel free to download and copy them, but I must stress that I am not a lawyer, and that I am not qualified to give you legal contractual advice, so please consult your own qualified legal advisor before you use any form, but hopefully mine will give you food for thought and serve as an example.

Please remember that a contract is an agreement between two parties and it is best if it is written down. For me the most important advice is that whatever is written down must be signed and dated, if at all possible.

I give this advice from my own cake business experience.

Cake Order Contract

This is best filled in with the customer or at the consultation. I would steer away from trying to remember the details and jotting it down on a pad, which could be mislaid.

If you take the cake order over the telephone you can email it to the customer, together with a confirmation of the cost and payment details, for their approval.

Ask the customer to check all the details thoroughly and reply with any amendments within a certain time confirming the order and the details. (I never allow any amendments to be made in the last two weeks prior to the cake delivery). Payment of the deposit secures the booking and acceptance of the cake contract/form details.

Being the 21st century you could have an electronic copy of this contract/form on your phone, tablet or laptop which could be saved on the internet in the cloud, which means it will never get lost.

The simplest way of doing this would be with Google forms.

Your cake contract/form will include all the details of the cake in terms of sizes (width and depth), number of layers in each tier, and fillings in those tiers etc.

All these details I have included on my sample Cake Order Contract/Form are on The Cake Biz Coach website.

I would also suggest a sketch or visual representation of the cake is included on the cake order contract/form. (A picture will do as long as it is of one of your cakes and not someone else's work.)

There are apps on the market now that will help you produce a visual representation of the cake, and stencils available to help you draw them out on paper. It is worthy of note here, that if the picture or sketch is on a separate document, that this sketch or picture needs signing and dating too, if at all possible.

A bit belt and braces I know, but I do know cake makers who have come a bit unstuck here with the customer questioning the design when the cake is delivered.

If the customer wishes to have a particular colour/shade of icing etc. on their cake, to match a cravat or dress, then a photograph of that item may cause a variation in the colour, so I always request a physical sample of the colour or material, in order to match it correctly.

(I had one lady who mixed her own buttercream samples. 7 different shades with a least three different colours making up each shade. Try matching those colours in a hurry!)

Always take a 50% non-refundable deposit for any cake or full payment upfront, except for wedding cakes when a final payment arrangement may be different.

I do try and secure a payment in full at the time of ordering as this saves me time and the effort of chasing the customer, who may have genuinely forgotten the final payment date.

You're a business, and time is money after all, and you could be doing other things to grow your cake business, and not eating into your 20 hours admin a week by chasing customers. (Remember those 20 hours were from an example I gave previously.)

You should be constantly looking for time savings in your cake business, streamlining as much as possible in order to grow your business and reach your success goals.

If full payment is not made at the time of the order, then I would insist on it being paid at least two weeks in advance.

If the full payment is not made then there will not be a cake, end of!

Do not let a customer pay for a cake on delivery or collection as this is opening the door to haggling or even worse.

State the time and date the cake is to be delivered or collected clearly.

I would inform the cake customer that the collection/delivery time and date is specific and no late collections/deliveries are possible!

I have been caught out a number of times with a late cake collection on a Saturday night, when I should have been somewhere else, instead I was stuck at home waiting for a cake to be collected.

One cheeky customer even rang half an hour after her cake collection time had passed and asked if I could drop the cake off to her, 5 miles away!

That one ended with her paying for a taxi to collect the cake. I tightened my cake contract after that one.

I know there is a fine line between dealing with a cheeky customer and a genuine customer in need, and how far you will go with your customer service is personal to you and your cake business, but I just thought I would mention it.

Customer service is key, but don't be taken advantage of.

Finally ask the customer if they know of any dietary requirements or allergies that they wish you to be aware of with their cake order. Now this for me is a 'speak now, or forever hold your peace' moment.

I have been caught out the day before a cake order was due to be collected with a customer telephoning me to say, could the cake now be gluten free as great aunt so and so is coming to the party and she needs gluten free !

Sorry too late, it is not possible.

The above is for mainly for celebration cakes contracts, but applies equally to wedding cakes with a few extra considerations.

Wedding Cake Order Contract

The same as a celebration cake contract except I would expect the full payment for the wedding cake at least 6 weeks to a month ahead!

If the wedding cake is being delivered I would include on this form the name and postcode of the wedding venue, together with a contact name and a mobile number for the person who will be receiving the wedding cake on the day, and more importantly signing for it on the cake handover form.

The mobile number is very handy, as I was once wandering around a hotel for over half an hour after setting up a wedding cake, trying to find the wedding organiser who was nominated to sign off on the wedding cake delivery and set up.

Once again time is money, and I hadn't charged for this extra time!

Cake hand over/receipt form

Whether it is a celebration or wedding cake you will need to have a hand over form signed and dated by the customer or whoever collects/receives the cake on their behalf.

Included on this form should be a guide stating the correct way to transport the cake, and how to unbox it. I would also include that I the cake decorator take no responsibility for the cake once it is handed over and signed for.

I would also include the temperature the cake must be kept at and if it can be refrigerated or not. This brings to mind another wedding cake delivery and set up I did, which was in a marquee, beside a lake.

It was an extremely hot day, and the set up was a couple of hours prior to the wedding. The marquee wasn't too hot whilst we were setting the wedding cake up, but I could see the sun was making its way around the marquee and the cake would be in full sun later on in the day.

When I obtained a sign off for the cake, I advised the recipient that the temperature within the marquee should be monitored, and the wedding cake moved if the sun did in fact continue to shine. It was the UK, so that was not guaranteed!

I hastily added these extra notes to the hand over form, and the wedding planner receiving the cake on behalf of the venue, was happy to sign the extra instructions thankfully.

Always leave an ingredients card in the cake boxes too flagging up any allergens and instructions as to any inedible items on the cake.

Another tip. I always take a video of the cake when I have finished setting it up. A full 360 degree video to show that it was perfect when I left it or it was collected.

Now I could go on for another chapter on receiving and delivering cakes but as I say it is best to take a look at my sample cake contracts and hand over forms.

I would also go a step further with my cake contracts, now I am a bit savvier and include intellectual property clauses.

You are a cake decorating professional, and as such you will not copy another person's cake or breach copyright, and you would not expect another cake business to do so either, but we live in an imperfect world where anything can happen.

If photographs are to be taken of your cake and displayed anywhere you must be credited as the designer and maker of that cake. You could even insist that the photograph be approved and watermarked first.

I would also get the customer to sign that this bespoke design is my intellectual property, and as such they agree that any pictures taken by yourself of the finished cake can be used as promotional material for your cake business.

Now I am being realistic here, and I know this may be a bit too much for your average celebration cake but not for a wedding cake.

I know a fabulous cake decorator who spent ages designing a bespoke wedding cake for a customer. She provided the wedding cake sketch and details of the cake etc. together with her quote only to find the customer did not proceed with the order. Some you win some you lose.

About six months later she was alerted to a picture on Facebook of the customers wedding with guess what, a very bad interpretation of her wedding cake design!

This design took time to create and time is money, so at the very least this hurt a wee bit.

I hope you take the above advice in the manner that it is given. In order for you to reach your cake business success you need to be professional and run your cake business as a well-oiled machine.

Copyrighting, Watermarks and Copying Others Cakes

If there is one issue that is Marmite (some love it, some hate it) in the cake business it is copyrighted cakes and copying.

I will outline my view for both and state that as a professional cake business owner, you should not be breaching copyright or copying someone's cake design without a correct license or permission!

Copyrighted Cakes

The list is endless but includes Disney, Channel, Louis Vuitton, The Walking Dead , Pudsey Bear to name but a few. All these cakes require you to buy a license.

Yes you do see Mickey Mouse, Frozen and Minion cakes all over Facebook, and you will continue to see them, but unless you have purchased a license/permission from their respective copyright owners you are liable to be sued by those companies.

Now if you plotted this in terms of a risk, I think the probability of you being sued is very low, but the punishment if you were to be sued would be very high in terms of cost.

I did have one of my Cakepreneurs ask the other day if unicorns were copyrighted, and to my mind I am sure they are not, so the current trend for Unicorn cakes gets my blessing.

Copying

Since the internet really took a hold and social media grew, cake customers are approaching cake businesses with pictures of a cake they had downloaded from the internet, asking to give a quote on the cake.

This is clearly copying and as a professional something I would not do.

But there are lots of cakes out there that are along a theme, such as the unicorn, drip or naked cakes etc. and the owner of the original design will never be identified. There are other cakes which are not bespoke designs either and the chances of finding the original designer may be impossible.

No, the copying I am referring to is the blatant copying of another cake businesses design particularly in the wedding cake market.

Therefore I suggest that when shown a picture of a cake you ascertain where they first saw the cake, and try to locate the designer and seek permission to replicate the cake from them.

Even easier is take note of the design, colours, materials and style and create your own design to complement the customer's cake request.

Now I find that most cake customers are fine with this and completely understand that as a professional, I will not copy another cake makers design if at all possible.

What really annoys me though is, a cake business or cake maker that use another's cake maker's image on their social media or web site and try to get orders using that image!

In order to protect yourself from this 'image theft' I would suggest that you place an intellectual property disclaimer on your website or Facebook informing others that the cake images watermarked as your own, on your web site, are the intellectual property of your cake business, and cannot be used or displayed by another person in any medium without your permission.

It really does upset me because I know the hard work, effort and expense some of these cake businesses have gone to, to design and photograph their cakes only to see them pop up on someone else cake business Facebook or website.

Therefore watermark all your cake pictures too. Watermarking It used to be quite technical nightmare to watermark your cake photographs, but now with the many apps that are available, it is so easy.

I am currently using an app called 'My Watermark' on my iPhone to watermark photographs, but there are many other apps like Livecollage available for free.

Now a watermark doesn't have to be in big bold letters, but I do suggest that a faint watermark is placed right through it!

Quite often you see a plaque or watermark in the top corner, or at the bottom of a cake picture. This is a photograph croppers dream that, they just edit your logo or watermark out of the picture.

So please protect your cake images with a watermark and an intellectual property disclaimer.

Chapter 9: Challenges

Scratch, Freeze or Buy and Business Continuity

I call this section on my attended 'Cake Biz' class lesson plan, the 'burn me as a witch' section, as the next few subjects tend to polarise opinions amongst many in the cake business.

The bake fresh, freeze or buy debates.

Firstly the cake mix verses mixing from scratch argument rumbles on in all the Facebook groups year after year.

Do you use all your own ingredients or do you use cake a mix?

I have worked with professional bakery chains, who supply celebration and wedding cakes, and most, if not all, use mixes. They trust mixes which they just combine with oil, water and eggs and know they will get a perfect cake every time.

I am not a big artisan baker (scratch mixer) as my cake collection was based on my cake decorating skills and my ability as a sugar craft artist. This is me!

You may be a cake specialist working to address a niche cake market, like macarons, or you may concentrate on artisan cakes, and I appreciate that we are all different, and I celebrate that fact, so therefore mixes might not be for you.

The reason I used, and still use mixes, is that I found the failure rate with my home (scratch) mix was a bit higher than I would have liked, and as a business owner I couldn't afford any waste. I have yet to have a cake fail using a mix!

It is also a fact that your cake customers may have become accustomed to the 'crumb' and feel of a baked cake mix in their mouths, if they have purchased cakes from any supermarket or large chain. Home mixed cakes tend to be slightly denser in texture and have a different feel to a mix.

Whatever you choose to do is fine, but if you haven't considered the time saved by using mixes, it may be time to take a look.

Cake mixes store well too. I always have oil and eggs in the house, as a store cupboard staple, so if I was to have a disaster, I can throw one together quite quickly.

The next contentious issue is the bake fresh or freeze one.

You are a business owner and as such time is money, and sourcing cake ingredients, carrying out a full clean down ready to bake, mixing ingredients, preparing your tins and washing up and clearing down afterwards is all valuable business time.

Try settling a stop watch and adding up how long it actually takes you. Obviously whilst the cakes are in the oven you can multitask and do something else.

Time is even more precious if you are still working in your full time job, and juggling launching your cake business with that job and maybe a family too. So baking fresh may be aspirational when you first start your cake business, but don't worry most of us have been there.

So you need to make a decision, do you bake fresh before every cake?

If your cake is due on a Saturday, as most cakes are, bake fresh cake business owners bake and cover with at least a crumb coat on a Thursday. If you have time I would go as far as getting your fondant/sugar paste covering on if you can on the Thursday to lock in the freshness of the cake.

(With naked cakes I put slices of bread all over my cake and wrap the cake fully in cling film and store in a cake box (not Tupperware) in a cool place but not the fridge .

Baking fresh may be one of your unique selling points so I am not going to dissuade you.

Freezing cakes and batch baking is a popular way of saving time, electricity or gas. I tend to fill my oven with at least four, if not 8 x 6 inch cake tins at a time and I have a large bowl where I can batch mix all the ingredients by hand!

I was used to working in a large bakery environment when I taught at the University, and they had large industrial mixers, so all I did was replicate this big batch mixing at home.

I mix by hand or use a hand whisk in the large bowl, with enough cake mixes in for at least 8 x 6 inch cakes.

I do tend to use cake mixes so emptying eight packets into a large bowl with the eggs, oil and water is very quick and easy. If you haven't got a bowl big enough, invest in one, a plastic one and a silicone spoon to make it easier.

Once the cakes are out of the oven and cooled thoroughly I wrap them in foil, then cling film and pop them in the freezer with a date and description label on them. When you want to use them, take them out, remove the foil and wrap, and place them on a cooling rack to defrost.

I do not freeze decorated cakes with their sugar paste covering on though. I did this once, and when I took it out of the freezer, it took two days to defrost and it was wet, shiny and sticky right up until the last minute. I had a fan on it for two days trying to dry the wet sticky surface.

I never keep my cakes frozen for more than a month personally, but they have been fine after 3 months. I have taste tested them with a fresh bake and no one can tell the difference. I freeze my buttercream too, flat in a big freezer bag so it doesn't take up much room.

My mixer will mix approximately 2.5kg of buttercream (2.5kg icing sugar and 1.25kg butter) at a time, so I don't mess about. If I need buttercream, I mix to its full capacity and freeze the surplus.

It's up to you, as it's your cake business, as long as you appreciate the time saving when you batch bake and freeze.

Next we have buying in your cakes from a good supplier. This is another method used by some cake business owners. If you have ever been to one of the big shows, like Cake International, you will have seen them there and perhaps tasted their samples.

Buying in your cakes cuts out the time spent on sourcing ingredients, cleaning down, mixing and baking etc. It saves on your energy bills by not requiring you to use the oven and the freezer if you are batch baking. This is a time saving way of running your cake business and is an option to consider. I know plenty of cake businesses that operate in this way particularly in the wedding cake industry.

Most cake supply companies deliver by courier, and you can order in bulk and freeze to save on the delivery charge.

Don't dismiss any of the above if you are serious about being successful in the cake business. All I ask is you consider them and go with what is right for you, your values and brand.

What happens when something goes wrong or unexpectedly happens is not something that cake business owners think about too much, if at all.

As a cake business owner you are, more than likely, working in isolation. Yes your partner or family may be helping with your social media accounts, or hopefully you have outsourced these and factored them into your pricing structure as part of your running costs.

But as far as being the cake maker and decorator, I'm sure you cannot ask your partner/friend to help you at the last minute. If you can, brilliant.

Therefore what big businesses call business continuity planning is key to running a successful cake business?

Hopefully nothing more drastic than a bout of flu or a poorly tummy prevents you from fulfilling your cake orders. Whatever the problem, or issue, that arises unless it is planned for it may cause you to work long hours and cause you a great deal of stress.

Don't forget you are in the cake business to have a lifestyle that suits you and your family, so long hours and stress is the last thing you need .So start as you mean to go on and build stress out of your cake business by planning for the worst.

Sit down with a piece of blank piece of paper and list every scenario that could hamper you from running your cake business, completing your cake order, or completing your cake order without the maximum amount of stress and anxiety. Put a vertical line down the centre of the page and for every issue you list, write a solution on the other side.

This is cake business continuity planning at its very basic level but it is a start.

You may be taken ill or unexpectedly called away. (I'm not going to tempt fate and list occasions when this may happen, but you can imagine). Your oven could break down or you have a power cut.

I spoke earlier about not seeing your real cake competitors as the enemy, but embracing healthy competition. I forged an alliance with a competitor years ago, and we did indeed share the odd cake tin or help out with a board or box, or two, at the last minute.

I never had the need to ask her to finish a cake for me, or vice versa, but we were both prepared to lend a hand if the time arose that we were unable to complete and order.

This may be a step too far for you, but please make it a consideration.

You could always train up a member of your family or a friend to step in too. One of my Cakepreneurs accepted a large wedding order an hour's drive away for the 28th December. She then became pregnant and gave birth two weeks before the wedding date.

I must congratulate her as she planned this wedding cake down to the last detail once she knew she was pregnant, doing as much of the preparation beforehand.

She trained her sister in law up too just in case there were complications. She also had another cake business owner on standby.

So ask yourself who will complete your order if you can't? Weigh up the risk to your brand of cancelling at the last minute.

Equipment failure is another consideration. I have mentioned insurance cover but your insurance isn't going to save you when your oven packs up and you have decided to bake a few days before the cake delivery.

Can you use another oven, have you got cakes in the freezer, or have you got time to order cakes from the specialist suppliers.

What happens if your freezer decides to break, or someone unplugs it, or you have a power cut and lose all your pre baked cakes. Again the insurance isn't going to kick in straight away so do you carry enough stock to bake again. This is where the cake mix may come in useful!

Go through all the scenarios you can think of and make a plan to mitigate against them. Planning is key.

Customer Expectations and Holidays

So you have sat down to plan your cake business year and when you will be releasing a new cake or cake design, and more importantly when you may be taking your annual holidays.

Please remember that to run a successful cake business, you should be looking to work less for more. You may have left a good career and stepped off the hamster wheel of commuting stress to have more 'you' time, or to spend more time with your family, so holidays are very important.

By holidays, I don't necessarily mean jetting off to the sun, although that would be very nice. I mean actual quality time away from your cake business.

"We pass this way but once" my grandma used to say, so let's enjoy it.

So I strongly suggest you factor in at least four full weeks each year, when you will be away and not working in or on your successful cake business. This is a minimum of four weeks as that is what you would get in any other job I feel.

You need to plan for these business holidays though, as your ideal customer may not understand that you need your down time, and from my experience may want to contact you 24 hours a day, 365 days a year.

I spoke previously about customer service and managing your customers' expectations of when you are 'open for business' and when you are not. You may not wish to publish the fact that you're away on holiday, away from your cake business, so planning is key.

Plan who is going to answer the messages on your web site, your emails, your Facebook messenger etc. Don't forget to limit the ways to save you time in business admin. Who will be checking these?

A bounce back messages that says 'I am unavailable until' doesn't really cut it as far as customer service goes for maintaining your high standards in line with your brand, so think carefully and plan.

You could use a virtual assistant (VA) service. This is very much a growth area. Most VAs offer a holiday package service where they will answer your calls and address any queries for you on social media or your website.

A VA service comes with a cost, but do not discount using one as you can't do everything, and a holiday should not entail you answering emails or even the telephone.

Success in the cake business also means a successful work life balance. Working yourself into the ground is not an option.

Remember to plan for your holiday too. Block the time out in your calendar and prepare your social media posts well in advance.

What happens if a big cake order comes in from a very special cake customer who you know will be good for your business?

This actually happened to me. I hadn't booked a holiday, I had just arranged with my other half to go away and he had booked the time off work.

This was a killer, and I was torn between my business, and my vision and goal of what success in my cake business meant to me. I can't lie, I did take the order as my other half is so understanding, but with hindsight I was wrong, I went against everything that I wanted to achieve and a work life balance was at the top of my list.

Going forward I always ensure that I book something now for my holidays, and pay I for it even if it is a Premier Inn or caravan by the coast with a no refund.

This prevents me from going against my vision as I'm sure I'm still not strong enough to resist temptation to work through my holidays.

I need to talk about customer expectations next and to be honest, once again I could fill a whole book with this subject, but I will mention a few that come to mind.

I have had the customers that have wanted me to produce a Minions or Disney character cake for them, which on so many levels was and is a no! Trying to communicate this is a nice way is always difficult, and in the beginning I did write myself a cue card so that I didn't get it wrong.

I would politely tell them that I was unwilling to do so as it was copyright infringement and obtaining the license for producing such a cake would make the cake very expensive.

Right on cue the customer would come back with the fact they had seen a Disney cake on other cake makers website or Facebook page, for which my reply was basically 'Oh I am surprised!

There is no way I would disrespect any other cake maker and question their professionalism or get into a conversion over it, so I would then outline the type of cake I could provide them with and talk about my unique selling points.

I wouldn't waste too much time on this conversation as the mere fact they had called about a licensed character cake indicated to me that they were not my Ideal cake customer, and that this conversion was not going to lead to a cake order 99% of the time. My ideal cake customer would have seen my cakes on my website, and a lack of character cakes may have given them a clue.

Another favourite is the customer who wants me to decorate their own cake, baked by them to some age old family recipe .Once again it is a no from me!

The cakes I use are produced by me to my exacting hygiene standards in my 5 Star Food Hygiene rated kitchen, and to use another person's cake (except for the one ordered from a professional cake supply company) is a risk. A small risk but even that small risk could damage my cake business, if it made someone poorly.

I also have a high standard in relation to how my cakes taste, look and feel and that is part of my brand identity, which I have worked hard to perfect.

Then there is a customer who wants a two tiered cake to feed 100 guests. Well I'm not a magician, and that is impossible. This is easily solved with the addition of a cutting cake which is undecorated.

Managing Difficult Customers Situations and Cake Deliveries

Let's talk about handling those difficult reviews or comments left on social media or as a Google review. Luckily in all my years of being in the cake business I have dealt with one!

A bad review and a one star rating usually follows a customer complaint that didn't go well.

Customer complaints again are rare but you never know and there are people out there who are professional complainers and refund hunters. But we are professional cake business owners and we have strategies in place to deal with these customers.

Firstly I find that having mapped out my ideal cake customer that I want to attract gets rid of those professional wingers and refund junkies who tend to be in the cheap cake hunter category, but not always.

If a customer contacts you with a complaint it may be due to one of two things.

The cake collapsed or has damage to it, or the cake didn't taste right and they want a refund.

Firstly let's take the one that crops up regularly on the cake Facebook groups, as I personally have never had it happen to me, but I have read about it too many times. The collapsed cake.

So you have made the cake and it is waiting for collection, or to be delivered.

My advice is to let the cake sit for a few hours, or even overnight perhaps, so that any instability will show up then.

Personally I have never had this happen and if you are confident with stacking and presenting your cake firmly on its board, you shouldn't either.

If the customer comes to collect the cake, I always box it up in front of them, and place it either in the foot well of their car, and tell them how to transport it. I.e. on a flat surface and driven very slowly.

All the details for transporting their cake, unboxing and storing it until used, are contained on the cake handover form that they sign when I hand the cake over.

I don't call it a disclaimer form as that has negative connotations. They sign to say they have read the instructions on how to transport and store the cake and accept full responsibility for it.

If a customer contacted me with a damaged cake complaining it had collapsed, I would ask them to return the cake within 24hrs to be inspected. The whole cake!

This would be the same for a customer making a complaint regarding the taste of the cake. I would ask that at least 75 % of the cake is returned within 24hrs for inspection and that the cake is preserved and wrapped up, if it is a complaint is about the taste.

As I say I have never had these issues, but I hope that this was because I was careful not attract the cheap cake hunters and chancers.

Once you receive a complaint, and hopefully you never will, then talk to the customer politely and professionally and try and resolve the issue .You will know if they are genuine or not. Badly handled complaints lead to bad reviews I find.

When faced with a bad review you unfortunately cannot remove it from social media or Google, but you can address it straight away in a calm professional manner. Write your reply clearly outlining your position on the matter.

It may be upsetting and so I always suggest that you ask someone not connected to your cake business, a friend or fellow cake maker, to help you pen a professional reply. Take the emotion out of the situation, and become a potential cake customer who may read your reply.

If you cannot delegate to anyone else then maybe sleep on your reply first.

Show how understanding you are, and that you are facing up to the complaint and not hiding from it. But don't bend over backwards as this may open the door for other professional complainers.

The bottom line is deal with it, don't leave it, as silence speaks volumes, and you have a right to a reply.

Be prepared, is always my moto, and to ease every eventuality, particularly with wedding cakes or tiered cakes that I am delivering, packaging and planning is key.

Don't forget failing to plan is planning to fail. Time spent planning can actually save time and prevent the last minute unexpected situations that might arise when you are delivering and setting up your wedding cake.

Here are some hints and tips for a smooth cake delivery process and remember to stop, breathe and remind yourself that you actually love what you do!

Planning your cake delivery.

Delivering cakes especially wedding cakes is a process is just like a mini military operation and needs to be streamlined. Plan, plan, and plan again, and be clear on what to do and when. Get your pre delivery checklist sorted by answering these questions

- The venue address and postcode and directions. Use a satnav or Google maps on your phone to calculate the time it will take and the mileage. Always add on a quarter of the time for traffic.
- Parking availability and restrictions. Actually drive the route and visit the venue if it is nearby. Do not incur excess mileage unless you can charge for it
- Make sure you have the venue contact number and a contact name and telephone number for the person who will meet you when arrive and sign off on the hand over form.
- Distance, how far you will need to transport the cake when you arrive at the venue from your car to the display table. Always do a walk through at the venue if possible. This reminds me of the three sets of stairs I had to negotiate with a four tier wedding cake on a very hot day on my own. Had I known this I would've bought another person much stronger than myself along to do the carrying. This was the early days.
- If the cake is to be adorned in fresh flowers make sure you have the contact details of the florist to discuss the flowers and the agreed time of delivery at the venue. It is best to work in unison with the florist. But read my section on fresh flowers before you enter into a fresh flower wedding cake contract.
- Always pack a wedding cake first aid kit. This includes extra fondant maybe royal icing to glue on decorations, extra decorations, wires and flower pics. A dustpan and brush is also a good idea.

Packing and securing your cakes to transport.

With your transporting a multi-tier cake or a cake with pillars the rules for transporting are all the same.

- Always transport the cake in single tiers if possible and construct cake on arrival.

- If you have to transport already stacked cake, make sure that it is not very tall and that you use a full cake box extender. Make sure the cake is dowelled properly at least 12 hours before transportation.
- Remove any toppings, sugar flowers etc. and place them in a separate box with tissue paper for transportation.
- Unless you have a delivery van that has a flat surface in the back, the best place to put the cakes is in the boot of the car or in the front passenger seat foot well with the seat well back. Never put cake boxes on the seat. No matter how flat you think your car seats are they aren't.
- To avoid the cake boxes slipping around use a non-slip mat in the boot. Yoga, exercise or silicon mats are really useful for this.

If you have far to travel and it is a hot day, and you haven't got air con in your car, or it needs regassing, then I always opt for an outer fridge box method. I construct this myself using frozen ice blocks like the ones you would use in a picnic hamper. I secure these firmly inside the outer box so that there is no chance of them slipping and sliding about and bumping the cake.

My biggest tip though, is allow more time than you think you will need to allow for unforeseen traffic problems on the day of a wedding cake setup .

Time management

One of the most difficult challenges of being a successful business owner, especially a cake business owner, is managing your time effectively.

You are a cake maker, a cake decorator, a social media marketer, a networker, a bookkeeper and finance manager watching over the budgets and profit margins to name but a few roles.

All these roles are very important, and are they key to success in your cake business.

Let's remember why you wanted to be successful in the cake business. Look at your goal and your vision of what being successful means to you.

If it meant spending more time with the family and being there when it matters, then you could find yourself drowning in cake business tasks and admin if you are not careful, and not achieving what you set out to do.

If this is you now, then step back and take a look at what is happening, and how far you are away from achieving your goal or actually living the life of a successful cake business owner.

Firstly ask yourself 'am I using my time effectively, and am I planning my time effectively?'

Remember I gave an example earlier of working 40 hours a week in your cake business, and I suggested that 20 of those hours were possibly not making cakes, but admin and marketing.

Take a look and see how you have actually proportioned up your time working in your cake business.

If you haven't started your cake business yet, it is a good time to plan your cake business tasks and perhaps 'time block'. Allocate the days and times for different functions.

Remember this is a 40 hour a week cake business that you may have chosen and hopefully by now you have chosen your business hours.

These business hours may, for the sake of an example, be 9.30am - 2.30pm to work around a school run. If this is replicated over 5 days then you will be short of 15 hours that week in your 40 hour cake business model.

(You may have chosen to take two clear days off each week, usually Sunday and Monday if you are a cake maker!)

Your children may be at home after 2.30pm and I do not advocate mixing business with pleasure. I promote being a partner and or a parent when needed, and be present in your cake business when you plan to be. Work life balance is key and never the two should mix.

Now it is usually those missing 15 hours that cause the issue when you are running any business from home or around another commitment.

Do you encroach on your cake business days off, and lose out on doing the things you want to do?

Or do you get up earlier, before the school run and use that time to make up your hours!

There is of course the matter of that we are cake makers and most customers want your cakes on a Saturday, so our Thursdays and Fridays are usually very busy. Do you consider putting the children in afterschool clubs on Thursdays and Fridays?

Add up the cost of having the children in an after school club verses the cost of getting someone to help you for a few hours on a Thursday and Friday. These are the types of considerations you need to think about when growing your cake business.

This is a business that needs balancing between the life you want to lead, and your journey to cake business success.

Maybe that you are still working full time, and trying to establish your cake business brand.

This means you will have more of a restriction on your working hours in your cake business, but it can be done. Carefully and with planning, but it is extremely achievable as most of my Cakepreneurs are or were working full time to begin with.

Make sure you have established your cake brand, and who and where your ideal cake customers are. Ensure that you are not serving the cheap cake hunters and that you are valuing yourself and your ability.

Then take baby steps to get established and plan your way to cake business success.

Time block your activities. Here is a suggestion for using your time effectively. It will not suit everyone but it acts as an example of how to manage your time in a cake business.

Example:

Firstly look at your emails and or message for the half an hour every cake business working day. Include listening to the voicemails from the previous day too.

(Hopefully you have managed your cake customers' expectations of your response times and limited your communication methods. That saves time hunting around on Facebook messenger, Instagram and Twitter Messages etc. For messages)

Respond to those messages and then walk away from the pipeline. Close them, done! Do not let your emails or social media message platforms steal valuable time from your working day.

Of course leave the telephone on during your cake business hours, but remember to switch it off when your cake business working day is over. (If you are still employed elsewhere during the day then leave it on answerphone and request they text or email you)

So next, hopefully it's 10.00am, and it's time for your social media catch up.

Allow yourself up to half an hour to check out your business social media, and like and interact with others on social media, via your business Facebook page only!

Do not be tempted to look at cats in hats, and your cousin's neighbours attempt at parking video on your own personal social media. No this is business social media time!

The time to check out your own personal social media is outside of your business hours.

Take a look at your competitor's social media, and at the pages of those who you aspire to be like. This is liking and commenting on social media time, and catching up with what is going on with your collaborators, and real cake competitors in the cake business world.

I have just described an hour of cake business admin that could be written into your cake business working day.

Hopefully you have already streamlined the above 'admin functions', and now have a more efficient morning routine, requiring less than an hour to answer queries and to catch up on social media .Now there's a target for you !

If you are starting work in the evening after a busy day job then just alter the time in the example, but still make the above your first tasks. Then close emails and social media down, do not let them distract you.

So if you carry out these two admin tasks daily that is 10 hours out of your 20 hour weekly admin time gone already, and there is still bookkeeping, marketing, and ordering to name but a few admin functions to fit into those 10 hours.

I imagine you are now throwing the book across the room saying what about customers asking for cake quotes etc. that is going to take me longer than half an hour!

Well the above example was to make your think, and yes it is too perfect, but a target for you to aim for. Be efficient with your time and know where it is being spent so that you can become more streamlined.

Consider outsourcing your bookkeeping or social media to give you more time to talk to your customers.

The above is just an example of time blocking, and time management but it is the key to the success of your cake business.

Let's face it a celebration cake takes about 3 hours on average, and a wedding cake 7 hours on average, so that's a maximum of two celebration cakes and two wedding cakes a week working with our 40 hour a week and 20 hour cake making example.

Once your orders increase then you will have to decide to either take on another pair of hands to help you with the cakes, or to outsource some of your admin functions so as to use some of the 20 hours admin allowance for your cake making hours, in order to grow.

One word of warning, and this is the 'false busy' task I mentioned earlier in the book in relation to designing a cake business logo.

It is very easy to get distracted with a task you are enjoying, and use up other valuable cake business time with a false busy task .i.e. taking a whole morning designing a logo when you could have outsourced this for between £5-£25!

Plan your time wisely for each task and stick to it. Keep an eye on your hours and time block to help your cake business to grow.

If you find you are having a quiet period then why don't you use this to produce your social media posts for the year and to network? Maybe look at adding other income streams into your cake business but be warned.

Ask yourself how long the tasks that are required by this other income stream will take you, and compare the revenue per hour for this other income stream with the revenue for a cake order.

Other income streams are great when you are quiet, but when you become busy with cake orders will they be stealing the time from the core cake business. Tread carefully.

Chapter 10: Let's get this business going

How Can I Continue to Support You?

So as we come to the last chapter and reflecting back on what you have hopefully learned, you are either in a corner of the kitchen rocking back and forwards thinking I just can't do this, or you are up for the challenge, and let's get started on your journey to cake business success.

I must add here that throughout this book I have tried to make up examples of cake business names for demonstration purposes only. I have exercised due diligence in checking that these cake businesses do not exist. The names referred to in this book do not relate to any cake business of a similar name worldwide, and any similarity is purely coincidence.

Finally do not let this book fall into the shelf help category, to be left on the shelf after you have read it .Whilst you happily or not so happily carry on running your cake business in the way you always have.

You purchased this book for a reason, and that tells me that you can do it. That tells me you have an appetite to do this, to be the owner of a successful cake business.

You may need to re-read the book, and I do highly recommend doing this now and again to focus you on the task ahead.

Plan out and manage your workload and don't venture into cake business overwhelm. Maybe sleep on the book for a few days and then start again a chapter at a time.

I truly want you to succeed in the cake business, and reach your success goal whatever that maybe.

There are very few cake businesses operating at the top level in the UK, and why shouldn't you join them as there is actually nothing stopping you. You can do it, all you need to do is believe, focus, plan and do it.

I can't push or force you, the vision and the passion has to come from you.

I am passionate about helping people to grow a successful cake business and not to be taken advantage of. I put my heart and soul into coaching people, both men and women in the cake business from around the world I have coached clients from Africa, Spain, France, Germany, Australia and the USA, so if you think I can help you please get in touch for a free no obligation chat.

We will talk about your cake business and the issues you have and I promise I will cram as much free advice into our call as is humanly possible. Whether you are in the UK or not, I can help you.

I can support you in so many different ways and I will hopefully ignite a passion and drive in you to take your cake business from good to great, or start you at the beginning heading straight towards cake business success.

I can also support you via my Facebook group where you can learn how to be a success in the cake business at your leisure instead of thumbing endlessly through Facebook at the cats in hats.

Join my free online Facebook group together with other cake business owners, or would be cake business owners who are eager for success. Just like and follow The Cake BIZ Coach on Facebook and also @Cakebizcoach on Instagram.

There will be lots of free learning in this group as well as lashing of help and support from experts and other cake business owners.

No question or issue is too big or too small .Don't forget I have a team of designers, brand experts, accountants and social media guru's to support me in order to support you. I want to give you the best advice possible and therefore I use the best advice and support and wrap it all up in one bundle to support you.

I am going to do my best to get you to be the owner of a successful cake business, but I need a buy in from you. A commitment that you will do all you can to make it happen too. So let's see what I can do for you.

You may already be running a cake business and need help with branding, pricing or social media or with hunting down that ideal cake customer.

I am continually trying to support cake business owners and I will be developing lots of free advice and guidance which will be posted regularly on my Facebook group The Cake Biz Coach.

Finally I have been writing this book for over 7 years and if it wasn't for meeting Abigail Horne & Sarah Stone from Authors & Co. this book would still be on my laptop, phone , bits of paper here and there but not published .

They are the reason you are reading this book today and I cannot thank them enough for their belief and loving support they have given me over the 6 months it has taken to get the book together.

If you are thinking of writing a book, talk to me about my experience, and I will point you in the right direction. I will help you get the support you need, but I am up for a chat about my book journey experience if you would like one. Anyone can write a book just ask me how.

Be warned though, the house doesn't get cleaned that often and you will be living on takeaway sandwiches and soup as writing is addictive, a very happy place to be. Seriously this experience has been one of the happiest of my life knowing that I can help cake business owners achieve their dreams.

Contact me now for information on how I can help you personally with your cake business or for help and advice on writing a book.

My Free no obligation discovery calls can be booked via my website at www.thecakebizcoach.com.

The call will be free and time zones can be accommodated.

Happy baking and cake decorating everyone and see you in my Facebook group The Cake Biz Coach.

Made in the USA
San Bernardino, CA
14 January 2020